HER PARAPHERNALIA

Her Paraphernalia

On Motherlines, Sex/Blood/Loss & Selfies

Margaret Christakos

Essais No. 1
BookThug 2016

Canada Council
for the Arts
Conseil des Arts
du Canada
 ONTARIO ARTS COUNCIL
CONSEIL DES ARTS DE L'ONTARIO
an Ontario government agency
un organisme du gouvernement de l'Ontario

Funded by the
Government
of Canada
Financé par le
gouvernement
du Canada
| Canadä

The production of this book was made possible through the generous assistance of the Canada Council for the Arts and the Ontario Arts Council. BookThug also acknowledges the support of the Government of Canada through the Canada Book Fund and the Government of Ontario through the Ontario Book Publishing Tax Credit and the Ontario Book Fund.

LIBRARY AND ARCHIVES CANADA
CATALOGUING IN PUBLICATION

Christakos, Margaret, author
    Her paraphernalia : on motherlines, sex/blood/loss & selfies / Margaret Christakos.

(Essais ; no. 1)
Issued in print and electronic formats.
ISBN 978-1-77166-234-5 (PAPERBACK)
ISBN 978-1-77166-235-2 (HTML)
ISBN 978-1-77166-236-9 (PDF)
ISBN 978-1-77166-237-6 (MOBI)

    I. Title.

PS8555.H675H47 2016   C818'.54   C2016-900644-1
                                    C2016-900645-X

PRINTED IN CANADA

Do thine own thing.

—MJC

paraphernalia: Arrived into use in the mid-17th century, denoting property owned by a married woman *apart* from her dowry, for example her own things...derived from medieval Latin, based on Greek *parapherna* 'property apart from a dowry', from *para* 'distinct from' + *pherna* (from phernē 'dowry').

[CONTENTS]

Étude 1 · Her Itinerary   · 9

Étude 2 · She Comes From Everywhere   · 23

Étude 3 · Retreat   · 65

Étude 4 · Chips & Ties   · 75

Étude 5 · Up Into Her Hole   · 93

Étude 6 · One Body   · 121

Étude 7 · (Iphigenia-as-) Siri, a series   · 133

Étude 8 · Cellphies   · 145

Étude 9 · Her Paraphernalia   · 159

Étude 10 · Cavort   · 199

Étude 1
Her Itinerary

thinking sh
was hers she needed to
get a handle on her own stuff
and soon wake the hell up honey

It is July 2012. I turn fifty. My daughter has recently turned fifteen. Earlier the same year, at the age of eighty, my mother has suffered an ischemic stroke that has deprived her of the ability to create or receive unjumbled language; she speaks a new language for which there will be no reliable translation. I have begun to interpret her facial gestures and the varied affective sounds she makes to alert me as to her opinion or disposition. Oddly, the words she has retained, from the difficult garble of paraphasia, are unmistakable expressions of her love for and pleasure at seeing my siblings, my children and me. My mother loves me; for the first time this is not a happenstance camouflaged by irony, sarcasm, aloofness and fatigue. My mother finds me beautiful; her adoration seems to bubble up to meet me, along with kisses and nuzzles.

I hold her hand and stroke her skin. I comb her hair. I assist with small tasks around meals and page through favourite artists' monographs with her as she oohs appreciatively, with recognition and appraisal, at examples of the visual art she has deeply loved her whole adult life, but with which she especially began to identify after becoming a practicing artist as her four kids grew to teenagehood and began, one by one, to leave.

I have never before had such physical access to my mother. To be with her in this debacle is to have her and be had by her, an original phase of my life as a woman, daughter and girl. I glimpse a palpable umbilical rope that moves from the middle of my body through the middle of hers and which extends toward the other women of her lineage, from whom I am descended, but with whom I felt little attachment or identity.

Growing up I had an easier physical proximity to my Greek father's mother and sister; they became my notion of physicalized matrilineal fundament. I could go to them and be hugged, comforted, fed, remarked upon. Far more than my mother's maternal British line, I facially resembled them and their kin; it seemed easy for them to embrace me. They loved me outwardly and let me know this.

My father's mother was infirm and delicate, often bedridden. Her husband had surprised everyone with an early death when she was fifty-three, and by the time I knew her she was perennially fragile, yet elegant, with graceful manners. I did not perceive her as a sexual woman, as she never remarried, nor did she seem to have had any subsequent romantic life after being widowed. Though she lived beside a freshwater lake, with a private beach, I never saw her in a bathing suit, nor even with bared calves. Sitting at the edge of her double bed or in her living room, I would stroke her skin and touch her hair. We shared quiet murmurs and unselfconscious hand pats of mutual affection.

My father's sister, after whom I was given my middle name Anne, after the age of fifty moved in a gradual expansion toward precarious obesity. I perceived her as having a large presence but no sexuality, or a sexuality that was arrested in a love of showy costume jewellery and brightly printed tent-dresses and capes, some velvet and fur-trimmed. There was indirect family lore about her life before she was fifty. A strikingly beautiful teenager and young woman, busy with church groups and her eventual elementary school teaching career, she had taken the apparently tragic turn of passionately falling for only unavailable men. A cousin, a priest. Like many daughters, she seemed to have been in love, in some overburdened way, with her own father, who reportedly adored and overindulged her.

By the time I knew her, her sexual body seemed blotted out of existence, or ballooned inside of gallons of soft proxy. Her dark brown eyes sparkled; she loved to take polaroids of me and my siblings, click, gah-zhoom. She did like to swim, paddling in a kind of slow breaststroke, head held aloft above the water, and I remember her sensual pleasure in the waves under glinting sunlight as her physical encumberment lifted into a bobbing, playful immersion in the lake I loved and grew up swimming in, as often as possible, my entire girlhood, until I left my hometown at the age of seventeen. I remember the wide breasts she displayed in the large bathing suit structure, which also had a skirt over the top of her thighs. I recall her arms and upper chest exposed to the elements, and her hefty figure emerging onto the beach, with her head and the manicured thick dyed-black curls arranged into a still-dry upward "do." I felt feminine kinship with her in our shared interest in the lake, but registered the truce she'd made with its possible pleasures.

My own mother did not like to swim. She didn't like the water, having nearly drowned under its shallow blue membrane when she was still a toddler. By odd coincidence her Anglo and American parents had rented the beach property on Sudbury's Ramsey Lake from my father's Greek parents, and she had stumbled and gone under the water, staring up through it for several minutes as near-drowners do, until someone (I don't know who) noticed and smashed her up into air again. As an adult she also reported having a kind of allergic skin reaction to being in the sun and after the age of fifty preferred to cover her arms, wearing men's cotton shirts with buttoned cuffs, diligently sealing in the cleavage area and upper chest as well. There seemed to be something foreign about physically exposing what my culture indicated from every other direction was suggestive of female sexuality.

Still, I knew she was a passionate woman. About her earlier life, I knew that in particular she had been an official lead fan of Frank Sinatra, organizing other casual fans with timely updates on sightings and personal goings-on and providing attentive micro-reportage of his international performance activity. She was also exceedingly generous in creating group spirit in her work as a bookkeeper. On more than one occasion as a prepubescent, I sat at our kitchen counter hearing her rehearse truly wonderful rhyming poems she had penned for her office parties; charisma and drive rouged her cheeks and escalated the velvet tones of her laughter.

She was intense, involved in her own manifestation, yes, but also maternally hell-bent and willing to stay up all night with me to make sure the last hookable rug stitch on a family studies project was in by deadline's dawn, or the last rhyming quatrain was secured on my (our, really) Grade Six epic poem about Jeanne Mance. I got the kudos at school, but knew the collaborations had been intimate, thrilling and worthy. She dutifully conveyed a puritan work ethic, yes, but also something more subversive: how the night's middle could serve art, above all, and that time was malleable.

While I was immersed in completing my own high school career, there she was, barely five feet tall, existing within one notable shimmer after the next, becoming expert in whatever new art vocation she took up, using her whole body to establish a ceramics studio in the basement, to complete late-night design assignments while she undertook a college visual arts program, to peel off moist hand-laid paper page after page of freshly stroked watercolour paintings. I remember her hauling out garbage bags full of gorgeous wool she happened to have on hand from her weaving practice—she had a six-foot poundable loom in the middle of our living room, and was obsessed equally by complex patterns of math and hue— in order to set me up to crochet my university boyfriend an entire blanket our first Christmas holiday apart. She seemed infinite.

At the same time she often seemed vehement and lonely, held in a silent marital standoff within our home, much as happened in my own marriage over its final difficult years. In her public life she was widely known for her bohemian originality, yet from a young age I had observed her obligatory tea-time propriety and daughterly agreeableness on visits to her British mother's large and decorous living room. By the time I was ten or so she was rarely a visitor to my Greek grandmother and aunt's small mainframe cottage. There seemed to have been a split, or many splits, and I felt these in my own confused fidelities. As my mother became more of a practicing artist, I longed to emulate her; but more and more I didn't know how to do that and to remain connected to touch and sexuality.

Instead, through my first decade of romances, I would get wrapped up in someone, some ordinary guy mostly, elevate him to sex-god status, and then complicate the attachment, whether requited or not, by becoming newly or additionally interested in someone else. It wasn't exactly a polyamorous inclination. It was in some ways a refusal to be limited, a mode of staying available. I liked the idea of being fluid and flexible, of migrating among various affections, and of rationalizing over and over that good love was expansive, exponentially propagative and the enactment of a kind of ethical plenitude in the world.

I also, though, can track a mini-history of enamoured mutual liaisons that veered toward an outcome of eventual unrequited sexual love. It was as if the movement from pleasure to the deprivation of the sexual love object was a turn-on almost more than any other factor. It was a diversion that led me to poetic writing, I see now.

From 2012 to the present day is three years. It is April 2015, and for most of the last nine months I have written barely a creative word, certainly not a word within the bleak and tumultuous midlife stage of my motherlines itinerary. In some respects the lapse in writing has reflected the state of shock and languagelessness brought on by the treacherously levelling end of my twenty-three-year-long partnership. Well, we raised three glorious children together; the heart lifts to admire all that was creative about the marriage.

At the same time I have been adjusting to the strange metabolic flatness of menopause. I have watched a small troughline form on one side of my brow, as if a miniature riverbed has been dessicated of the clear-flowing stream that used to replenish automatically. Truant are the peaks and valleys of my mood chart. Almost gone—for the moment—are those spontaneous tremors of turn-on that always characterized my physical life; now if I stop and notice a sudden moistened charge in my groin, it may be with as much scientific inspection as bold, unedited pleasure.

I am only fifty-two. These emotions seem like they should belong to a woman in her seventies or eighties. But no, now I see, to become fifty as a cisgendered woman can mark a scraping off of sexuality and subjectivity that, no matter how much prepared by a hurrah feminist intentionality for agency, operates like a self-aware social trouncing. Did my mother feel these losses and erasures as she entered her sixth decade, sleeping separately in the house, all of her children entering adulthood, myself at age nineteen involved in a serious live-in relationship in Toronto? I saw my mother as vibrant, full of life and rich in community, eclectic, powerful, a small electric ball of opinion, always changing, actively learning, fearless, driven, unsleeping, free. I did not identify her as lonely, or ailing, or missing sex. I didn't have such words to attach to the older women of my family, although it seems day-plain to me now that nobody was getting any.

I felt their looking upon me, though, as if my luck would be unconstrained. By 1979, I was poised for movement—away from northern Ontario's provincialism, toward the frank chaos of contemporary art, a metropolitan life in Toronto, the freedom to explore lovers and garner sexual attention. When at twenty-two I told my mother I was going to marry the man I had made the blanket for—even though she was very fond of him—her pallor dropped a few shades. She asked, wasn't I a little young? Always discreet, she did not argue aloud for me to protect the unlimited future she viewed me as having as a young female artist, but her tone was clear. I would be making an error.

It's true that my development as an artist was starting to be vibrant and daring. Along the way I took creative writing courses, especially one with bpNichol that deeply influenced my open-form aesthetic, and recognized a talent for the poetic. I had pleasure in being before audiences, hosting small groups into aroused aesthetic encounters with language. And I slept with a woman and recognized that my experience with staving off monogamous clarity was rooted in a deeper desiring multiplicity, that I shouldn't delimit my location, where I might go, and how I might come.

That early marriage ceremony was deferred, and my mother's awareness that I was bisexual prompted a muting breakage between us that never quite got addressed, although a novel sprung from the erasure. Sex from that point was better undiscussed; its intricate details were unnecessary to share; something fuzzily self-shaming had entered my identity when I went back to my hometown. I have written about becoming unreadable as a poet whose language work (or "play," as it is so often diminutized) seemed too experimental to paraphrase or organize with conventional literary legitimacy.

But homophobia was one of the underlying silences, that can go fallow when bisexuals arrive at a visible primary relationship status with a heterosexual partner. Easier for others to label lesbianism as a lark, and me as an experimentalist, only. In retrospect, I entered life-changing love relationships with other women before my common-law marriage with a male partner and our immersions into parenthood, and continue to be drawn to both male and female partners. That I am still outing myself in a text like this, advancing a self-portrait that includes my desire for women and women's bodies, repeats my sense of invalidity. But it is necessary to understanding why it is that I needed to somehow write and exist as a writer throughout the years I raised my children, nursing them, holding them, nurturing them physically while sensing a chaotic lack, a split, a stark breastlessness with my mother and all of the other women in my lines. I couldn't touch them, and aside from by my Greek Nana, I had not felt touched. Decades of sex did not seem to repair that lack.

Mom's break with speech forced the conundrum to the fore. If we couldn't use language to stay at our designated endboards of the non-touching field, if we now had to bring close our eyes and hands and skin to communicate and understand each other in the most basic sense, what other openness might I begin to feel in finding connection to my transgenerational motherlines? It is humorous to me that whenever I type this word on my keyboard, the machine slips in another s. *Motherliness* is the materiality woven by these lines about my mother, her mother and the other women forebears I have been attracted to know. Like the intense entwining of bodies I experienced while mothering my own children into language, an illness that caused the erasure of language (and all of language's deployment of distance between bodies) made the lush beauty and tenderness of my mother's body appear to me, finally, and mine to appear, ineraseably it feels now, to her.

When I began this project what I loosely knew was that all four of my grandparents had arrived from elsewhere: Nanny from England, Grandad from Upstate New York, my father's father from Molaos near Sparta, Greece, and my Nana from a small mountain-backed seaport village on the east coast of the Peloponnese. By 1915, they were all residents of the Sudbury region in northern Ontario, separated from their birthplaces, new immigrants, shaping their imaginations of what would become real to them, each cleaved from the phantasmic memories of where they had come from— where I come from. Not compelled in my earlier decades to do so, I decided to travel to the small coal mining village of Radstock in Somersetshire, where my mother's mother Dorothy had been born, seemingly on the move toward Manchester where she lived through to adolescence. I wanted to go there, and then to Liverpool, where with her mother and brothers she had boarded for Canada in 1914 at the age of fifteen. And I decided to visit the small port village of Kyparissi, to richly embody fantasies of my father's mother Demetra, and her forebears, to envision the specific rock, water and soil—her cultural grove—that had held her so firmly to the earth until she was sent to marry in Canada, in 1915, at the age of sixteen. They said she was older, of course. I recognized the parallelism of my two immigrant grandmothers arriving in northern Ontario within a year of each other, each in her mid-teens, embarking upon a reproductive itinerary whose disruptions and dysfunctions would shape my very existence—and that of my own daughter, also fifteen when I began the process of discovery in 2012. I wanted to consider what of their pleasures and tumults of self, what textures of loss and self-composure, could be brought along through my writing subjectivity as a series of "études"—"tumultétudes," in fact—messy portraits, porous forays. I tried to consider in a very personal way the idea of how we as women think about seeing ourselves appear in the world, not solo, but enmeshed in each other's overlapping

19

appearances, creating for and with each other a form of choral "coming," of rippling into presence, and of imagining both a past and a future that connects us.

I don't know where future decades will move me on the map of partnership, but my post-married paraphernalia includes the new glint and calmed jangle of my mother's skin close under my fingers, with less fearing love for her, alongside what I have embodied about my grandmothers' girlhoods, and what I have been able to summon about their mothers and other women in our motherlines. Whatever they lost hold of sexually after the age of fifty, their bodies have come alive to me, aesthetically and with incessant rhythm, as lakes shift, and wind moves, and language undresses and confesses and curls.

this is the year I started to this is the year I finished with
this is the year I collapsed under this is the year I took a
shortcut to this is the year you this is the year we this is
the year near a body of this is the year someone forgot my
this is the year months were this is the year girls this is
the year seniors this is the year baby boomers this is the
year corporations this is the year rivers this is the year
magnetic this is the year care relations of social media
this is the year dark hideaway bars this is the year
caesurae this is the year plump bedding this is the
year invertigo this is the year mutancy this is the year
continuity obsessed this is the year pituitary this is the year
headstone this is the year little pebbles this is the decade of
the year counting backward this is the year odours this is
the year muscles this is the year tantric ludicrousness and
ludic tantrums this is the year smartypants this is the year
cleavage this is the year alphabet flipped this is the year
unremunerated this is the year victoriana this is the year
watermelon juice this is the year important this is the
year cross-legged this is the year scrape this is the year
fast black minxes this is the year emergency exit window
this is the year hover this is the year memory-smoke this
is the year roaring this is the year writing went all free on
us this is the year nobody this is the year weeks this is
the year eyebrows this is the year hand on stomach this is
the year linen this is the year alphabets lipped this is the
year keynote this is the year uncoverup this is the year
parkwalk this is the year chortle this is the year spill off
edges of earthly this is the year pandemic kaleidoscope
this is the year shiver this is the year leg-shaped this is
the year every twelve minutes this is the year feelings in a
series this is the year touching in a series this is the year

reframe this is the year put your mind on a back stoop and see what cats come round late at night to drink this is the year futurelack this is the year unstoppable affection this is the year hula this is the year total crosswalk this is the year polylinguist parrots this is the year transparent parents this is the year in real life this is the year simultaneity this is the year deliberate this is the year numb baby finger this is the year tenderloin with apples this is the year thinking in a series this is the year loopdeloop this is the year nothing this is the year despite this is the year erasure of self this is the year implode upload this is the year how do we know what if this is the year aglisten this is the year strict structure this is the year pageflap this is the year fielddepth this is the page yearstuck this is the year sniffing this is the year fall away from your expectations people and breathe this is the year homilies this is the year broken news feed this is the year public squares this is the year alcohol this is the year dream-choke this is the year my this is the year lost this is the year last this is the year fester this is the year best this is the year list this is the year luster this is the year lust this is the year cost this is the year untrust this is the year kissed this is the year pressed this is the year plausible this is the year leave you at the train this is the year train this is the year you this is the year not so fast asshole this is the year retro this is the year globalized care relations this is the year idea of ideas this is the year cervix this is the year wait this is the year wait this is the year wait this is the year unsegmentable this is the year sound editing this is the year truthcape this is the year excavatory gestures this is the year cake stand this is the year yearning this is the year.

Étude 2
She Comes From Everywhere

So you see yourself in several mirrors. So you see yourself. You see
your body and your face. You face your body and see your face. You
see yourself in mirrors in washrooms in airports. You have a look
that seems squirrelly. You look at yourself and appreciate how bad
the lighting is. You look at your eyes. At your cheeks. You see a wide
silver realm of mirror all around your little head. Do you exist? How
old are you? How many years have you been here? Is this the first
time you have arrived?

If you stay here for an hour or two who cares? If until the afternoon
people might walk up to you. No they will not. You are alone here.
You are alone not able to see yourself unless you go to the bathroom
mirror and inquire. How old are you? Are you fifteen years old? Are
you a girl? Are you a woman? Do you have the attributes of your
sex? Are you a fake? Will anyone walk up to you? If you were fifteen
someone would walk up to you and ask if you were alone if you were
all right if you knew how to get where you are going. But you are not
fifteen, are you?

Absolute rubbish is what the woman says. You watch the woman
poking with an erect index finger into a handheld device. Prodding
for someone else to see her. T-o # s-e-e # h-e-r.

There was the first mirror in Pearson. There was a little mirror in the
airplane washroom above the sink where I lingered for quite a while
to stretch my legs and clear my nose of phlegm. This is a private act.
I can see myself in the mirror committing such a private act and I
like knowing that I am not seen. But comes the thought quickly that
a camera might be monitoring the airplane washroom. Certainly
there is a camera. There is surveillance in every nook and cranny of
an airplane, surely. I want there to be surveillance and I don't want
there to be surveillance. I cannot decide what I want. I look in that

mirror and taste my phlegm. Now why do you have to make a note about that. Are you a child? Are you a woman?

For many months I have been reflected by you, my mirror. I have watched you with my corneas and my irises. Which part of the eye does the watching? Why don't you know anything? Your little head and the big silver realm around it.

I have been in this country an hour and already I have stopped myself three times from asking for help. Three separate people. They were perfectly positioned to be instruments of my order. First, the lady with the Kleenex, and I could not ask her for a Kleenex. Phlegm was gathering outside my nostril like syrup, the plane was landing and I could not ask her. How stupid would you sound? How presumptuous? Why should she give a Kleenex to me, a total stranger whose body was revolting? Then I did not ask fully about the way to get to central London. I asked partially, twice. I could not hear what anyone said back. Why? Suddenly deaf? Suddenly invisible? Do I exist? Am I fifty?

Is it reasonable to think that Virginia Woolf examined herself every fortnight or so in a mirror and thought, crap I'm huge and shimmering. What did she look like at fifteen? Everyone is fifteen at some point unless they go down like a tragic consumptive. I was fifteen once. I looked in the mirror and thought I was small and that I was required to smile whenever anyone looked at me, or when I looked upon myself. You look attractive when you smile. So that is one way to be in an airport. Keep grinning and you'll remember your youth.

For quite a while I have not seen myself in a mirror. Am I alive? Do I exist? Am I a woman? Everyone over there is in the same green T-shirt. They are a club or a team. They recognize each other and then it is clear who they are. What am I wearing? Who cares? I have a lot of people who love me on another continent that will have to suffice for now if only I can hold such a vast silver realm around my little greyed-out head.

Here in England it is almost noon. In my body it is 6 a.m. It is 6 a.m. Am I fifteen? Would I wake up for school soon if so? Did Nanny like to go to school and in her room was there a mirror? Did she take her photo to let her girlfriends know what outfit she was wearing that day? Did she post herself on the public Internet? Why can't I get online here at Heathrow fucking airport, two thousand and twelve. Get real. Am I real? Clea, are you stirring yet and will you count the morning in your mind's eye to yourself, here here is the first day my mother was gone from me for her writing trip. I am alone. I have my girlfriends my aunts my other relatives I have my teachers and my Facebook page. I have 600 friends. I have a huge shimmering head in the middle of a small blue frame. I am up to the challenge. I am fifteen and I exist.

Are you awake as yet and have you Googled to see if she exists? She had a few thoughts of your face your cheeks and top lip. She begins to recognize that maybe you have forgotten her for a moment yet you love that she exists.

Is love a forgetting?

[Photo note on fb #touchingseries photo, posted July 2015] arms / Clara Griffin Merwin and her daughter Grace Clara Merwin (sister to my grandfather); "Photo property of Clara's mother Lucy Griffin"; Clara is my great-grandmother. "Picture made at Beaver Meadow farm, north river, New York."

28

If   I   am   looking   for   you I   will   look
       into   covered   spaces.   Look   close   up
&   still   blurred.   When   you   have   children
you   pass   most   of   the   day   looking
at   them.   You   love   to   look   at   them
       you   have   to   look   after them   you want
to   watch them.   Your   eyes   fill
       with   your   children.

walked to Covent Garden + did some shopping. bought T-shirts for kids,
arranged to have them sent to them—bot pr of shoes—went to Covent
Garden Piazza + watched some performers—guy in gold suit sitting on
nothing! + a guy pretending to be a puppy—very funny—went into Royal
Opera House + bot ticket for alternative opera program Sat night—went into
Piazza again didn't know what to eat + wandered until ravenous—had steak
& guinness pie

In the courtyard with a turquoise pool shuddering and rippling at the wind raking it. Urns with cedar and bright small blossoms. Trees and the bushes have been trimmed. You are full from a full English breakfast. You ate well. You did not overeat. Good on you. Hard when it's all-inclusive, feel you should get your money's worth. Pack it in. Pack it on. Pack it away. Pack it. Pack. Did you eat enough? Is there enough love for you to see your own contour? Is that your ass upside-down in that mirror? Yes it is a good ass. Pretty fine ass ready for the boulevards of high school.

If you arrive at the restaurant and no one offers you a table, follow one waiter with your hawk eye and pull him in. On the far side of the room is the woman and her mother. Fifty and eighty perhaps, Italian, quiet, facing each other. They are on an English vacation. The daughter arranges for her mother to be brought special items, yoghurt and cheese, not on the full English breakfast menu. I say fifty but perhaps she is fifteen frozen in eternity. Women who do not move past GO. Women who are fifty and fifteen looking in a mirror and saying wait Mamita, I'll speak to the maître d'. Both have bouffant hair sprayed in place; complexions smoothed over by creamy cosmetic. But here I look at them as if they are bodies and faces and how is it I do that like any man?

You think you are different and then you see yourself in the mirror and you know you are pretty much part of a continuum and nobody cares if a mirror says exact or inexact facts about your fatness which is guaranteed. Women are fatness. Fat is fact. Fact is we are all so fat we don't fit in the elevator together and must go in one at a time, solo, and be carried into oblivion.

My my doesn't breakfast make you morose. Morose and remote. Remote from the others eating and how do you wipe your nose in public? Let alone sneeze. It is impolite to rock a sneeze in a public restaurant or math class. You cannot let your blood leak out in the cafeteria. Cannot flash any stains of your liquid self in case the others notice you breaching the obligatory dryness of the body. Shake your booty but let it suck in its own mess.

Are you awake yet and have you Googled her to see if she exists?

Do you have a day at work or a day at home and how many times do you touch yourself. She starts sentences not thinking they will wander into the.

Something annoys her.

bus to Hampstead Heath + went to John Keats House then walked into woods—kitefliers on Parliament Hill—view over London—walked down to bus—could not get on—no change—weepy suddenly—went to café called Kalendar—had meze platter + latte—hummus tabouli tzatziki + baba ganouz—one falafel + pita—then got C2 bus all the way down past Camden Town + Regent Park to Victoria Stn—walked to palace—in St James Park along pond—lovely—came to mall + ICA—had martini—got shiraz for Barbara—film by Christian Petzold abt East Germany 1980—beautiful—lovely—walked up to Chinatown—had beef ho fun + pork dumplings—streets alive with thousands of tourists

The splashing rain under tires, rain splashing under tires, tires spilling rain upward, is very English. You can exist in your room without coffee without the Internet access code for a while longer. You bathe and douse and spread a few substances into and onto. In the mirror you look pretty and blatant and woggly and resolved. With your hair wet your face looks about five. Fat little five year old who gets a kiss on the breast that nursed all three of the children for a total of five years. You did your time, body.

A window and a mirror. TV and a laptop. Camera and a book. Magazines and maps. Plug sockets and plugs. Lights that light up to tell you what to do when things are ready what is half-charged or fully charged. And the splashrain spilling up from Southampton Row. Everybody driving here or as if in a mirror.

The children have not written emails to you. On the first day they did. By the third day they are taking it for granted that you are away in new places and they are at home. They are at home. Good. Fine. You are the one gallivanting. Are the woman at fifty wondering whether you exist or if you are fifteen or five.

If you came to London in the mornings you might have walked through St James's Park, fed a duck or swan, seen the palace, walked the same heath where I saw couples and babies and dogs and kitefliers knifing their kitestrings higher. The British Museum Parthenon installations and Royal Opera Hall's shimmer Covent Garden's stalls and St Paul's courtyard. Victoria and Albert would have meant something to you. But before WWI, so it is in the envelope of a century coiling over to a new era, before catastrophe shredded all notions of boys apprenticing in their dad's shop and gradually learning the trade, taking over, virgin marrying a virgin and beginning an upward-bent family economy. When you were five what did you think you'd be doing at fifteen? Did you think you'd be moving to Canada? Did you know? Did your family speak about the idea of it?

When she was twenty-five or so my mother came here to London to see its intricate empire rainsplashing up against the side of hotels and park gates. With her girlfriend Margaret, after whom you are NOT named. Named after her sister Margaret who was Peg née Merwin Hewson d. 2012 and her mother Dorothy Margaret née Cowcill Merwin d. 1990 and her great-grandmother Margaret née Livsey Henson d. 1931. In between is her grandmother Amy Sophia née Henson Cowcill d. 1971 after whom you, Clea, are named. How is that, well by your middle name Sophie. So there is a laceweave of naming and of who is five and fifteen and twenty-five and fifty for we all carry all those selves our entire lives and it is not chronological.

Not chronological.

Did you Google eGgloo elgooG me this morning and was I still asleep?

Do I exist?

If you exist and there is a small river winding with thistle crowns sprouting from its embankments. I am speaking here of the inside of your theatre your balustrade and upper balcony. Knees. Your knees.

woke late—stayed in room writing + loading photos till 3 went by bus to Tate
Modern + saw The Taming of the Shrew at the Globe. had a light supper
before + walked across bridge, took bus back to Holborn stn. lovely day

woke 7:30 a.m.—loaded photos from yesterday + went down to breakfast,
packed + took bags down at 11—went for hourlong walk around
Bloomsbury till 12—returned to hotel + got stuff—at Paddington stn bot
ticket for Bath (visa)—got sandwich + water + train—arrive 3 p.m. in Bath—
couple of hours in room on wifi which is GREAT—went for walk took some
photos—came upon a nice pub-restaurant called Rose + Crown—got pint +
fish + chips

Yesterday was a mirror of its day before and then also something completely original. So original in fact you did not have words for it or could not find time to find words for it. In transit. The young guy dressed in designer duds with brightly coloured striped socks. Kept flashing his ankles. Oh his ornate ankles. Not a mannish area often shown. Glances, stripes. Colours. There's a lot of segmented green and hay colour and lime and some blondness creeping into the visage. Manicured meadows and sudden-come sheep and lambs. Trolloping mares. Meres.

More rows upon rows of flattish blond walls which set off windows and doors as important portals from the inside to the outside and back in again. The extravagant hydrangeas pinking the walled gardens. Up and down hilly parts.

You figure there's a room and how different is sleep in any room. But sleep is always as different in every room as being awake and walking is in any day.

When fifteen I couldn't sleep and now at fifteen she can sleep pretty well. Clea, you sleep well on most occasions and now whenever you are asleep I am probably awake and when you are awake and walking I am perhaps asleep so. Do you getmymeaning? We can convene in the splice between awakesleeping as if in a massive pink hydrangea room of air. Isn't that fun? Did you think I had forgotten?

I joked on Facebook I was taking Nanny for a walk in her pram tis 1899 she's six months old with a cherubic little face looking up at perhaps her mom Amy Sophia who is how old? Have to check my notes. Have to hit the pave. See Bath. Go. But I am dawdling hoping you will be awake soon and we will touch screens as though mirroring ourselves through words here. I am wearing your shirt and Mom's bone bead and ruby necklace. Do you see me? Do I exist?

I begin to tally what it is to arrive in Bath's stuccoed, maroon-leafed Britishness. Recognize much of Dorothy's aesthetic in this little town, especially the palette of her notion of grace. I'm starting to develop some skill with making a photo chronicle portraying myself at fifty travelling alone. I'm trying to recognize myself photographing myself, instead of creating depictions of how I should feel for others. I've equated being in a photograph with delivering a picturesque smile. Now I'm accessing and allowing a calmer self-portrait, marking and mapping my movement through waves of being alone in time after mothering intensely for nineteen years. The camera—a device that I had developed almost moronic incapacity with in Canada—is becoming a little machine-companion through which I can sense narrative intersections among being a granddaughter, a daughter, a woman, a consumer, a traveller, an aesthete, a writer, a sensory being on the loose...

Today also occurs this idea that solitude unfurls one to see oneself, to begin to pitch self both here and there, to create a screen to sit on both sides of. Perhaps there were two weeks. Two weeks across an ocean when she Demetra saw herself both sides of this unfurling screen. Family left in the village, groom to collect her. Two weeks on a rollicking ship across entire an continent of water. Her unsealed vestibule for just that solo time. Did she look in a mirror at existence. Did she shimmirror. She is fifteen, unmothered, about to bride. Did the unknowable excite?

The voice in your head swivels volume over the day. Into the evening. On the boat she hears she hears she hears. Is it erasure. Sraeh ehs sraeh ehs sraeh ehs.

And now the volume of love swivels winnows not rises but troughs to a vacant cavern of a beat that should have an echo but produces none. You thought to throw the wedding ring in the canal. Would it be regrettable or trulygreat?

You listen.

[Photo notes, posted later on fb]

Bath Public Library. Marriages registered in April, May and June 1898
Daniel Lever Cowcill, 1898; record lists his district of origin as Chorlton (Manchester)

Dorothy Margaret Cowcill April–June quarter, 1899 birth on record
Clutton district of Radstock.

walkaround Radstock a bit + take some photos—museum opens at 2 so
I go over to hotel for lunch—ploughsman's board w/ honey ham salad
+ bread, coffee—over + over news bulletins about missing five-year-old
girl—now expected murdered—police ask public to no longer be involved in
search—so as not "to contaminate" evidence

She exists, though not in registries extra to the microfiche. This little mining town alike the mining town where Dorothy alit. Coal and timber. You stroll and get caught up in the churchyard's fecund desire to commit existences to public record. Slabs. Coffinframes. Salutations. Last gift to the beloved is the alphabet. As humans leave we offer them the alphabet to carry them over a kind of river. Imagine the storehouses of letters rotting at the boatman's ankles. H-i-s # s-t-r-i-p-e-d # s-o-c-k-s.

Cedar arches and crabapples a menstrual red which reminds you of how many more times you will issue this. Across the Atlantic fifteen year olds begin an itinerary. You envy. When Demetra arrived she was expected to be of age, to become efficient at reproduction. She disappointed. Loosed one loosed another loosed another. Bad host. You recall loosing one loosing one loosing another loosing another. In the churchyard there are branches arching into a green canal and you float through.

You don't know where to look in the stones for whom or why but to be a person is as good here as any spot. The crust that separates above from under. Her under. Present from passed. Your boots stew in the leaf slide and muck. Inside the boots are feet with skin on them.

Are you awake as yet and have you Googled to see if she exists?

She begins to hallucinate your molecules. Sounds better than it feels. Vapidity sifting into the uncertain. You have a job and pillars of time to upprop. You… concentrate on the unbounded.

Headed out at 10:30 this a.m., from my lodging in Bath, so I'm rounding hour eleven. It's been good exploring the town my grandmother was born in, and seeing more evidence of the aesthetic that shaped her and her signature décor years later. My bus ride from Radstock to Bristol took me through about eight eighteenth/nineteenth-century villages, all overgrown with masses of verdant foliage. A hilly curvy secret ride; God knows how the driver remembers where to turn and turn again on this self-erasing route. Bristol train station is one of these huge cavernous Victorian-feeling places that England's known for, and the train is high-speed, comfortable and on schedule. Too bad it has been night the whole way so no view aside from pulling in and out of numerous stations. While on board I've gotten to download and edit photos from the day in Radstock. Feeling pumped, having taken a few risks in the face of uncertainty today and in each case arriving at some happier more interesting circumstance than I would have had I gone a safer or tighter route. And I'm oddly thrilled to have been in the place on earth where my maternal grandmother breathed her first breaths.

This is a train are windows as mirrors ricocheting your image cancelling the geospecific surrounds. Who cares for it is night. You will slip into Manchester in a dark cloak and sidle up to a hotelier. Will get there. Fifty. Some were loosed sure but some were held and bornbornborn into the beaioutifull alphabet.

Why don't we spell it that way, hey.

[Photo note, posted on fb]
Granny holding me, 1962. My maternal great-grandmother Amy, John Street, Sudbury.

38

[Photo note added later, posted on fb]
I had only been on my trip for ten days but already I found myself drawn to graveyards in a new way. The one in this photo is in Manchester, which I found en route by foot to the Levenshulme area where my grandmother's girlhood home was. This particular cemetery was shattered, and looked monumentally untended. Sloppy trees and little creeks crossmapped the capitulated grid of fallen headstones. For about an hour I stepped carefully through the broken graves, reading names, dates, reasons for death, small accounting of lives. I didn't encounter anyone else, tourist or local; I poked around sensing a connection to past generations uncommon in my sense of things. There was a quiet breeze and sun crackling my gaze. I didn't know why I was there. I knew why I was there.

[Combined photo notes, from those posted on fb]
A stunning sunny day, in the lively market just north of the Levenshulme neighbourbood, with its Victorian bones. Conceivable the large Anglican Church I pass about eight blocks from May Grove could have been her childhood church. A train track over-passes just behind where Nanny's house is, and I note how her relocation in Sudbury must have felt familiar to her, with such continued proximity to the railroad. Ah there it is, 1 May Grove, at the end of the row. Original iron gate.

[Photo note, posted on fb]
Fifteen-year-old girls at shopping promenade. I asked them if I could take their photo for my daughter back in Toronto because I thot they were beautiful and they blushed and laughed and said okay.

Liverpool—Cavern Club lover—brave aberv evarb—then the outing—
breakfast in the hotel + tip—lunch at Marine Museum. Beer bus to Albert
Dock, walk back to hotel—Albert Dock stunningly vast + well designed
integrating historical + contemporary elements—St George's Hall—
Biennale + historical jail + court exhibits + concert hall, contemporary art
installation by Romanian artists—Marine Museum + Archives—Intl Slavery
Museum—Lunch at Marine Museum—Tate Modern with beer at Mellow—
walked by CHRISTAKIS Greek tavern. Plan to meet M at 9 p.m.—wet for
him (again).

[Photo notes, posted on fb]

Grade Ten art students. Fifteen-year-old girls outside Marine Museum.

New regard for the paintings of ships Nanny had... never before related
them to her cross-Atlantic travel when a girl.

This is basically where my grandmother Dorothy Margaret Cowcill boarded
her ship for Canada, to arrive June 1 1914, age fifteen; grateful to be here.

London—woke tired 8:10 a.m.—took too long having shower + trying
to connect with Internet + get packed—didn't leave till 10—got advice
from doorman to take cab to Green Park stop and metro to Heathrow—
unfortunately Heathrow Express was the one I needed from Paddington—
got too late to airport—had to buy new ticket from Terminal 1—Aegean
Airlines. Luckily the flight cost was still only $235—I can try to get taxes
back on the British Airways ticket. Had food + a coffee—+ a beer—used the
instant Internet machine 3x—went from feeling really quite stupid + upset to
more patient + resolved

Arrive by night, sleep for seven hours, wake brain-boggled to my courtyard at Plateia Karitsi. I email the children for virtual hugs.

[Photo note, posted on fb]
Oct 12 Athens. Men come to the window for the playing of the anthem.

Walking in Athens my first morning, bewildered and anxious at my adriftness without English, I think of how Mom's stroke produced a sudden sleight of tongue slipping away all recognizable signs and sounds, replacing them with unreadable untranslatable glyphs. Before leaving Britain, I'd asked M while we were still flirting about the parts of his Algerian-Russian childhood he'd experienced in Arabic and Russian. "Who were you, who are you, when you think of your past? Are you the same person in your first languages as you are now, in French and in English?" He said, "I don't change who I am, I am continuous," and then seemed to be willing to volley some of the differentials, before we simmered into what seemed to be inevitable and intense *physical* speech, lol. But somehow I wondered this about Mom; did she sense how she existed in her past, before the loss, and was it anything like how she existed now? It still seems unassessable.

My first Greek coffee, in the National Gardens, a little bitter with grit inside and creamed by milk. Mixed currents converge in me: grief and affection for Dad, who I miss badly, finding myself here in a kind of pilgrimage to him, and daring a taboo consideration of his body, his self, his sexuality, his intelligence, his machismo, his kindness, his physical beauty, his youth, his assuredness, his separateness from me, his masculinity apart from his skill and commitment as a father, his strengths. Back in Liverpool, my new friend had described to me his international job as a technical inspector of energy facilities, making site visits to monitor the security of hydrogen membrane away from chlorine as brine is converted to usable energy— surveilling for any sign of leaks, which can be lethal. It occurs to me that intimacy with him offered a rare lens on considering my love for my father slimly membraned apart from lust, in this case, for a lover who looked like him more than any other partner I've had. A fleeting navigation, two nights, oddly still in England where my British heritage was also being poked and prodded, which also gave rounds of touch that repair and redirect the solo traveller's lostness and looseness and internality.

From the café, I stroll through the zoo area, with creatures that seem abandoned, past a Greek couple tossing eggplants in at mangy mountain goats. There's a lovely old gentleman pushing a toddler in a stroller, and when I see him a second time he is whistling like my father used to, sonorous and capable, life-filled. I walk through the park to the exit across from the presidential house where one soldier in army grubs is wiping the sweat from one of the military guards stationed outside the gated house. A non-stop line of tourists gathers to take a selfie beside the guard and the poor guy looks to be about asleep. A small boy pretends to stamp-march like the guard has done, on the spot. I set off down the hill and come to the Panathenaic Stadium marking the site of the first Olympics, and encounter the first of many clogged intersections streaming with men on blaring motorbikes, cabs, buses and cars. The motorbikes zoom across every lane and between lanes of car traffic so the whole mess buzzes and roars organically. I have my first glimpse of the actual Acropolis up on the hill over the gardens and National Congress. I cross at the lights, daring all the weaving bikes, and go down Olgas to the temple of the Olympian Zeus and the Arch of Hadrian, stunning archeological treasures plopped amid or rather surrounded by traffic and streets that seem to pinwheel off in many directions. Here there are more stunning views of the Acropolis overlooking the city and for a moment I feel like fainting. When real experience hits the imagination's longings something in the body wants to go virtual again. Almost 3 p.m. and I stop for my first meal of the day at a typical Greek restaurant, sit outside under the tents and have a Mythos beer, bread, Greek salad (fetaccompli, I joke to myself) and pork souvlaki—which comes with potatoes and rice exactly as in a Toronto food court. I ask for a side order of tzatziki and sit eating for well over half an hour, during which period two young girls individually come begging, the first about seven, saying "You are beautiful" to every tourist woman and showing lighters to buy, followed by "10 cents please," all the while costumed in a heart-sobering grin, and then later a ten year old plays a toy accordion—some famous Greek song—and asks for money. The same unflinching public smile. I can glimpse ahead graff all over the Plaka. Around me, other white tourists stream through the stone-bricked street, moneyed, mobile, like me, watching and gauging reality and history, luck and privilege, charity and complicity.

You are not so sure you exist and others insist. Others make a claim on your behalf. Relatives vitally strive to mesh you into worldviews that account for you. You struggle. You wriggle.

You are sure you exist and others resist you. Others tear down a lineage. Relatives veer from your frame and blur it. There's no accounting. You hiccup. You apologize. Maybe links exist and you postulate the ifs and whys.

An angle always lingers to be noticed. Your attention gels the others. You exist while they exist. A narrative imbues you all with meaning that tastes a little like an orange.

They are not so sure they exist and others insist. Others make a claim on their behalf. Relatives vitally strive to mesh them into worldviews that account for them. They struggle. They wriggle.

They are sure they exist and others resist them. Others tear down a lineage. Relatives veer from their frame and blur it. There's no accounting. They hiccup. They apologize.

Maybe links exist and they postulate the ifs and whys. An angle always lingers to be noticed. Their attention gels the others. They exist while they exist. A narrative imbues them all with meaning that tastes a little like fields and fields and fields of oranges.

Acropolis. Oct 14. 9 a.m. at the Aeropagus; perfect light. Slick marble stairs. Men; cops. Thrilled to be at the Odeon of Herodes Atticus; note the "ode" in Odeon. Theatre of Dionysus. Me at said theatre; proof. More proof. Note mountainous horizon. About 30 degrees; perfect. Aeschylus, Sophocles and Euripedes… flitting around. Ah the beautiful caryatids… copies, but did see four of the originals in the Acropolis Museum later. Women do this every day. The marble glistens from wear; Dad would have liked this I think. Parthenon. People everywhere, all quiet and respectful; rather stunning. Ongoing reconstruction. View down to Theatre of Dionysus. Bloody hot. Blew my mind. Gorgeous structure directly below Acropolis. Whole edifice built on 94 columns, allowing the excavation of the medieval and Classical remains below it; amazing. No photography allowed in Museum; entire collection awes. Café on third floor; had rapini, black-eyed pea and smoked trout salad; spectacular. Hoot. Glass panels floor the courtyard allowing visual access to remains below; looks like water.

Women; Marble. Oct 15. Gotta get past the cops first. I'm in. Sphinx. Meanad in the middle. From Eleusis. Artemis with deer. Earliest Nike. From Eleusis. Mother and child. Mother and daughter. Aphrodite. Demeter. Kore. Demeter and Persephone. Eleusian mysteriac rituals. How good you were, dear daughter, c. 420 BC. We know how you feel. Ah, let's let him stay. Three. Tragique. Demeter. Artemis. Aphrodite. Siren with characteristic plumage. Let's get closer. Siren. Siren. 15th-c BC, mind you. Psi types. Louise Bourgeois, hello. Figure. My cups runneth over, bronze. Night time outside the National Archeological Museum. Woman. Woman. City, 2012.

Good acoustics. Oct 18. The scorched hills of Sudbury c.1915 would not have looked so unfamiliar. Corinth canal cool-eo. The urge to sign in. Corinth. The Corinthian Acropolis. Graff exists. Pulling into Mycenae. Katerina, our guide, very good. But this is MY picture of the Lion's Gate. Walk on thru. You're looking down on the Argive Plain out to the ocean. But this is MY picture of the Treasury of Atreus. Who knew that beehive soared so. Humans like to make monumental structures within which to feel specific and contoured. Oranges. Coming into Epidaurus. Walking toward the theatre. W. O. O. W. View from the top seats is STUNNING, yep. Little fish swimming in the bay at Napflio; my first contact with the sea here. Where the executioners resided. Dap-sparkle sea. Check out the cathedral up there. Byzantine church near the port. Trees outside hotel. Everybody has to get up at 6:45 a.m.

From Napflion to Delphi via Olympia. Oct 19. Again with the scrubby hills. Courtney and John. Around Megara. Harvesting wind in Arkadia. Lagnite-burning plant at Megalopolis. Our driver Stelio. Around Tripoli. Freddo stop. Graff exists. Katerina the human encyclopedia. Temple of Zeus at Sanctuary of Olympia. Temple of Hera, and behind the Phillipeon. Judges' spots: hellanodikai. Priestess of the goddess Demeter gets a spot (only woman allowed in the sanctuary). Stadium, 6th-c BC. Arch entrance to the Krypti, 2nd-c BC. Olympia Archeological Museum. Men, masks. Woman, shield. Half and half. Griffins. Siren. Winged bronze female. Drive from Olympia to Patra. Rural scenes. Toward Patra, entering the mountains. Stunning Patra. Driving along Corinthian Gulf toward Delphi. Near Napfaktos; no, that's Nafpaktos. Ascending Mt. Parnassus to Delphi, view from hotel porch. Cool '70s-designed hotel, chalet-ish, Old Delphi.

Beauty ruins. Oct 20. Waking up in Delphi. Not a bad day. Pythia. The 17 of us and then a bunch of students from somewhere. 8:45 a.m. at the Temple of Athena; way way up Mt Parnassus. Was a tholos. To the Sanctuary of Apollo at Delphi. Eleanor, Anrundam, Dee, John. Try to absorb the layers; the air is thinning. Omphalos, omphaloessa; hey, Tim Whiten, I get it. Temple of Apollo beside the Rock of the Sybil, beside the laurel tree (to the left, unpictured). Katerina explains the subterranean ethylene swirl supposed to have intoxicated the pythia; pssshaww. Altar of Apollo; upper sign says people from Chios get to jump the queue. German choir students sing a capella at the theatre to the god of music Apollo, 4th-c BC. I think the oracle's trying to tell me something. W. O. W. Now I have ascended to the area overlooking the theatre. We weep at Delphi; at Delphi, we weep. Try to absorb the layers; the air, ever thinning. Continue to ascend to the stadium. Many curvy paths later. What feels like a country road toward –. Here I chant love is life; life is love –. Very thin air, very very high, unimaginable a stadium would exist here –. Here's the stadium, immense, utilitarian, seems suddenly the perfect place for a race. Wish you were here my loves. I invoke you. Katerina uses visual aids. Apollo and Artemis. Athena. Really big sphinx guarding the Rock of the Sybil. Female figure in motion from Temple of Athena. Another omphalos. Three dancers. Charioteer. Bob and Kay. Lamb stew with spaghetti; hey, Dad. View from restaurant, looking to Corinthian Gulf. Look, Dad, I'm at Thermopylae. Pasiakos resto. Now that's the way to do up a restroom. This is the scale of dessert I feel most comfortable with. Driving to Kalambaka, 2.5 hours. Lamia. Trikala region, much drier and scrubbier; stay tuned.

After a couple of days on Mykonos, swathed in sun and sea, I return to Athens ill and need to go comatose for a day. Finally I emerge from my little studio room. I am hesitant and mute, deflated by my inability to pick up any natural use of Greek phrases beyond "Efharisto." Even "gay-says"—or as I refine it later, "yah-suhs"—totally stumps me. Rarely having travelled in non-English- or French-speaking countries, I am struck by how potent the silencing is when faced with a 360-degree surround of a foreign alphabet, a non-gridded urban plan and a dominant tongue that overpasses me. I don't feel inauthentic though—just quieted. I haven't caught hold of the thread that connects me to Nana here. Women seem to be second fiddles, to recede behind an ongoing procession of men, practically all of them attractive by my standards (although very stern and somewhat erasing of my gaze), who rule and wheel through the streets, walking, on motorbikes, in cars—they are everywhere.

I'm not even sure if Nana ever came here to Athens when she was a girl. She may well have gone straight from Kyparissi to Spetses—and then to France. Perhaps it was her nephew Spyrou who suggested to me when I met him in Montréal, along with his wife and daughter, that she'd left from France. All of the oral narratives I've heard by Greek women of the early 1900s describe going from Piraeus to Naples and Lisbon en route to Ellis Island. Given how there was no road into Kyparissi until the late 1950s, and travel literally happened by donkey, I doubt she would have ever gone outside the Peloponnese.

[Even once I make it to Kyparissi and have direct, translated access to relatives who can connect me to some of the details of my grandmother's girlhood and return in the mid-'30s with my father and aunt, I am too stupid and shy to ask for clarification and detail

48

on so many subjects. I am half-frozen in silent speechlessness for almost the entire time I am in Greece, well over a month, with a rigid overblown smile and inner shakiness. I am also in my body, in my skin, almost ecstastic, with recognition.]

[Photo notes, Oct 2012, posted on fb, as Album]
Sparta Oct 26–27, 2012. Hotel Nana, Near Larissa station, Athens. Ktel bus station; you try and figure out where to go and buy your ticket, go on. Uh uh. In the far corner, 19.50 euros cash only will get you to Sparti. Keep scanning. Lakonia; right on. Little studio apt in Sparta, my *sparta*ment, 25 euros; went out for the evening with very nice host Kostas and another studio dweller Adam, from Portland, who will next go work on an olive oil farm in Cyprus. Sunday morning kaffe. Sunday morning o.j. Mount Taygetos view out my window. Out for my Sparta walkabout. Do I look LACONIC enough??? Orange tree. Outside museum, closed for OXI Day. Graff exists. View across from museum. Museum. Oranges. Delapidated ironwork porches. Pomegranates.

u recognize
u recognize ur kin
u recognize kinds of letters
u have your bottle of water
u identify the front of the bus

it's a station
u know this

i heard ur voice on the internet
birdsong or a fist it
moved me

she wants me 2 buy a flashlight
wants 2 sell me a pack of kleenex
no i say over n over north american
no

natural forms will tell u where 2 walk
they r the commodities that sold u besides
in ur knapsack is the map

50

There are voices mulching the foyer from its quiet echo to a
staccato amplifier. I am already in my little bed.

I went to Sparti's outer ring of potholed roads.
CHRISTAKOS appears in Greek on signage; I could read this.

I got a lot of great photos.

Hundreds of girls danced in the traditional Greek style.

Taygetos mountain ponderously hovered behind.

In the thinking process I use my body recedes to a.

[Photo note, posted on fb]
Fifteen-year-old girls, in blue shirts and short school-uniform skirts, arms
interlaced, dancing in synchronized bouncing rhythms, lightly sweating,
smiling, giggling into each other's hair, while all of their parents, an
enormous crowd watches on.

A colossal limestone female head

R u awake as yet n r u on Facebook so we can stay in touch? R u fifty
or fifteen? U have great skin. Can I Google u. Can I friend u. If I tag
u will u confirm

She comes from everywhere, so where she comes from is everywhere, so, here, there somewhere everywhere. She comes. She'll be coming. She's about to. Circulating at the edge of a mountainous eventuality. All go out to precipitate her when she. Riding six white (goats, probably). At the juncture, she. Go out to greet. At fifty a female of her species and era. Yes we'll all round the mountainous eventuality for she'll be coming when she.

Left right climb left. Circle back. Right mount steeply left switchback. Veer left then right circle back. Circle back circle back left right circle back. Accelerate. Slow. Accelerate slow circle back. Gun engine pedal to the metal stick it north slide right circle back. Shortcut left swerve, squeeze it, swerve circle the tight hairpin lookout point quick right hold it hold accelerate fully circle then circlecircle circ cir circle—brake. Slow slaw slew sloo slou release gear coast down.

Do you have a day you want to remember alongside this day when you first come here around the huge mountain of it all—family history, Dad saying, don't go there they'll kill you haha, aunt saying wear your ring, others saying why bother what's this some kindaroots thing, lol—do you have a day you want to remember alongside this day?

Still I don't know how to speak Greek. I don't exist in this language. What is that white patch out there in the water, a school of fish maybe? Is it squid? How do I make sense? Sun on my bare back heats me from where it comes round the mountain, her mountain, mine.

At the shore is where the water meets her, yes I am sure. Perforates lacerates penetrates, no, where it meets her. Heels knees thighs groin groan oen oon oun and so on it's all precipitative. Plus sun beats down on plus sun soaks down in plus sun bakes plus sun doses insunimates. Sun plus sun plus sun plus plus pulse. She's coming round. S'mornin. Up sun up.

You see that white cross up there—pointing high behind a
prominent limestone outcrop—S says, that's where many villagers
died when the Turks came, 1820s, they were all hiding in that cave,
and some guy, I don't know why, turned them in

55

you'll see in the cemetery—there's one grave for all—a small grave
full of good human bones, I saw, those old sawn
and he was apparently pushed
to his death—the traitor, the one who told—
from that cliff *I gotta admit it's a*

horrific picturesque finish

then in ww2
the Paralia schoolhouse was used
as a POW holding spot—but
many of the villagers were in the
mountains, high, deep, hiding out, starving

I wonder if
they still heard
the sea I wonder
if they despised
the sea a bit
for those years

I saw a movie the other night in Athens, Defiance, about Polish Jews hiding
in the forest forming communities—I watched it with Greek subtitles, picking
out single words, clumsily fathoming all I find foreign; everything

Dad and I used to go driving around the Creighton hills outside Sudbury—
mountainish hills denuded crusted in slag all black + shapely make the
prettiest sunsets—car engine gunning sounds oceany shiny gold hood of
the Suburban (pre-SUV) glinting and always his smokes

amid Kyparissi silence
a bin scrapes, is scraped
metal whacks, is whacked on metal
shore surfs
surf shores
a little dapple portside
like aquiline tongues coming
to chat

and you are full of voices
no such state
as silence
we all know this and then *yep*

die

Am I a mountain? Am I fifteen? Does language come round my brain into my being and request a pass at the deathdrop? Yo, can I slide through, tonight I'm pretty tired and need some whiskey. Can you heat it for me, death? Will you warm my bedclothes?

If you are alone in a country where you are the speech-mangler, some kind of fog or mist burgeons on the fourth morning. Makes you feel rocky, like a hill covered in scrappy pine bushes. What happened to those trunks that they hug the ground? They don't want to lean too far out over the gorge. To exist stay tucked in the upper chest, an uncoughed cough.

A low-flying plane today brings echoic images of air attacks during the war and how villagers hid in the mountains and stayed as grounded as possible as the dark asterisks dove and roared. I find my imagination is limited by cinema. I really hate cinema some days. You know that when I say villagers I mean men, women and children. Shoving their roots into a ground tucked under the visible surface. Wishing to be inside the earth, as far from sky as possible. This is as human as the ones doing the bombing, for what, what, to own that land, to run that country? To be the villagers?

Land is the thing wanted. Land is the thing we come round the mountain for, to settle, to proliferate, to live a life. But nobody wants to live alone in a village. A village is a voluptuous multitude.

You awake over the oceany push and you Google to see if she exists

You xs and xs together for some smatterings of timesplice

you just know
when the writing's aflow like this
bp's about

BP in Greek
Something like VR

he's vriting in me
vrisiting my hand—vrisible
listen there's his tongue
portside
bportside

I lovr him infinite
how he's a real
greek graek griek griok griuk
oomun aswell all those tongues
comin vround
in circles

Sounds good. Through the roof maybe. Some way to lift it all skyward. But who wants to be in the sky. Maybe everyone. For who wants to be where they are? You?

Catch you on the other side. When you wake up in my time zone. When I ache up. Must be dreaming. I am in a tune. I am caught in the music. Thm ooosic. Looos. Bopping fidget ing ing with a beat as you know it's imposs. Thinking goes outha windoh. I don't know if the sheep downstairs appreciate it. Baaah.]

[Photo notes, posted on fb, as Album]
Womenexis. Oct 31, 2012. Toula Vourthis, daughter of Pericles, my Nana's
brother b. 1903, who so kindly came by today to show me where Nana lived
and to bring me to meet Thea Froso, here with Stella Vasiliou my expert
hotelier cousine!! View of the hills behind from the Menexis home. This
view just gives a sense of how they could see the sea directly. Birthplace
of Demetra Spyrou Menexis, 1899. The raised terrace now abuts a roof
garden from the ground floor. Front door grill. Bit better view. Terrace leads
to this staircase down to courtyard. View from courtyard. Thea Froso, who
was my father's first cousin, three and a half years younger, and played
with him and Tasia for the whole fifteen months they lived in Kyparissi
1937–38. Froso is Demetroula's (Demetra's) niece; her father is Nana's
brother Ioannis (John), born immediately after Nana, in 1900. Just a few
buildings away is the Hotel Paraliako, built recently but very coherent
architecturally with all the older homes. Stella and her lovely mom Sophia
Prontzos Vasiliou, who runs the Myrtoo apartments a few steps away.
Dining room at the Paraliako. Stella advises me to walk to the Ai Gorgios.
Path winds up behind the strip of homes to the side of the port. Climbing
up the hill and following a path along the side of one of the big hills. Really,
we could be in the canyon behind 381 Wellington. Lovely feathery furs and
pines. Bush with an acorn structure. So many reminders of Sudbury, ore,
granite, uncanny. Person fishing. Blues should be much more turquoisey.
Sudbury, no? Lots of birds; at one point a distinct growl, saw some scat.
If a doppelganger gets me please know I loved you all. Aristides, you did
a great job settling in Sudbury. A couple more shots of Nana's house from
across the way. Pretty much beside the main church. Homes built at turn
of century or earlier, would have been here when Nana was born. Great
spooky olive trees. Cemetery behind church. Ghosts in sheeps' clothing…
happy Hallowe'en.

S's snapping branches from the garden
preparing to plant new bushes such a lovely young woman
to run a hotel I wish I
ran a hotel

travel unravels me plants
me a new plot
is life real do
I love who I
say over and over
I love it's all
evolv

a valve
vivid edge of authenticities

her mom S says I think this deep love makes
you're a "real" Greek woman

[blush]

[Photo note, posted on fb #touchingseries]
July 2015, from Auntie Ann's scrapbooks "Red Hibiscus like those in
Grandma's garden in Kiparision, Greece." Assembled probably when Ann
was 27 or 28—1950 or 51.

Clea, it's funny when Maureen posts on a picture of you that I look really happy and great. It's as if for a moment you are my happy and great self and well I am over the hill, seriously. But Maureen didn't mean it that way. It's the way I take it, because of the culture that's raised me, praised me only for being fifteen and young and happy, and not a self-recognizing woman of fifty. I am fifty. Hey, Walt, you'd mean something else by this, eh.

I hear from Thea Froso via Toula that Efrosine my great-grandmother had not fourteen but sixteen children, and that nine of them survived. There's no mention of a faith culture that requires women to be a willing vessel or that expects men to take sex whenever they wish it. This is just three generations back. My great-grandmother was pregnant and pregnant and pregnant and pregnant and pregnant and pregnant and pregnant and pregnant and pregnant and pregnant and pregnant and pregnant and pregnant and pregnant. Fourteen times, for there were two pairs of twins. And of these offspring she lost seven. Only slightly better than a fifty-percent success rate. Think of it. I can barely think of it. Somehow the question of a woman's pleasure in self-recognition, both sexual and intellectual, evaporates in the barrage of sheer labour that must have strobed her corporeal reality for those many years. I can't even imagine if she liked sex, or Spyrou's returns from the sea. It seems indulgent beyond decency to ask this of history.

We contain multitudes. Walt meant something different by this, also, eh.

Given that Nana was the eldest girl, and sent away to marry, I can imagine now this displaced her from becoming a lifelong surrogate mother to her many siblings, released her to become devoted to her own offspring. It's hard to imagine Efrosine would have schemed to send Demetra away, given her workload. But away she went, at the age of fifteen, and, by fifty, her two surviving children were twenty-six and twenty-one. Here I am at fifty and my children, so far away from me for just this envelope of exploration, are nineteen, fifteen and fifteen. Ostensibly I am more bound to maternality at the same lifestage than she was. But I know my access to sexual and intellectual pleasures at fifty—and experiencing and examining their relationship to self-recognition—is the fuller bounty, the bigger part, of this legacy.

And in so many concrete terms my own basic freedom as a woman of history is coiled into this inspired decision by Efrosine to send her daughter to marry in a new country. It feels juvenile to recognize some of these things, and yet, it has taken me five decades to create the required conditions of recognition. As I share them with you now, at fifteen, from your outlooking threshold, I wonder what you'll make of them?

[Photo notes, posted on fb]
Nov 5, 2012. Elementary school in Kyparissi; older kids have to go live in Molaos Mon–Fri to go to secondary school. Toula brings me into Nana's home. The window sills are original, more than 115 years old. As is this cupboard. This fabulous picture of Nana hangs in the room; she must be about 14, before she left for Canada. Theodore is able to translate for me and Toula, and so we share stories and info. Toula says Efrosine's father was a housebuilder and did much of the work; the ceiling is original. This first-floor space would have been where the livestock was; the living space ran the length of the top floor (it is now two spaces and I saw the one side). Theodore points out the well. We go to Froso's—Toula's sister's—house, and some photos are shared. This is Nana's younger sister Polyxeni. Uncle Mike and his wife Katina, also from Kyparissi. Polyxeni in front of the family home. My godmother Joyce. Hey that's me! wearing those super-wide jeans that were popular for about two months...Nana, Aunt Barbara, Mary Argeropoulos and Aunt Polyxeni, and Mary and John's two boys— at Sudbury at the lake. Mike and Katina's wedding in the village. John, Aunt Barbara and Joyce. Toula and Theodore translating notes on the backs of some of the photos. So very kind. I'm not leaving.

And you are the one who needs the water's speech.

It's   hard   to   be   by   the   sea   and   write   63
about   anything other   than   the   sea.
It's   hard   to   be   anything   other   than
by   the   sea.   It's   hard to   write, it's
          anything   other.   It's   sea. It's   hard to
be   by   anything   and   write.   Other
than   by   the   sea   it's   hard to   write.
The   other   woman   left.   She   was   far
          over   on   the   other   side of   the
beach.   Who   was   she?

Feb 8, 2016—Realizing Nana had a cluster of losses much like my own—
Efrosine died February of 1946—so, Nana was 47—her father Spyrou died
September of 1952—Nana, 52—and her husband died May of 1953—she
was 53—in my case, end of a marriage, but the impact, the density…

You definitely exist. You shimmer. You don't need a mirror.
Mirroar. Sky. Myrtoo sky and sea and you exist.

Did you wake and Google her, did you recall her there in another
time zone? Do you love and why not love more? Amourrir.

Are you fifty or fifteen or five or a blend of interannum markers
mapping your procession to this terrace?

You come to the narrative space laid out by women whose bodies
are bones.

Smatter some, take a bone grind it groan grain break it to seed and
swallow.

There is a woman below me up early watering her garden of
bougainvillea and oranges. Mother or daughter. Pretty nice life
but if you come in the soft times don't imagine for a minute the
opposite cannot seize hold. It is not chronological. Our good
fortune is a blip

and permeates.

Étude 3
Retreat

When you arrive back in your hometown at the beginning you think it's all such an impenetrable mirror that there's no use in imploring of it any more slices of self. If you exist anywhere you are also erased there. No permanence. No unfragmentary self-image. In this saturated chasm you curdle into and out of yourself, blooming on a screen, quickly splotching to a pattern of smudges. Voices in the café rip strains from your thought-curtain. The Coltrane they play brings you back into your throat.

There's lostness and retrofit in how the images of travel slide against everything normal. Maybe having the known to return to is a harbour; or maybe it's a poor replica. Maybe it's an incaved gut; or maybe it's some sort of inflation that could get dangerous.

One of the abysses of writing is not knowing where to go next. A café can help with its walls and something to buy. You recognize the transaction ringing you up into an economy at large. You are not so outside that you drop into a meadow. Existing gets the proof of a little receipt and a slowly dwindling glassful. Fact is, anywhere your body arrives requires social space to prop it.

Anywhere your body arrives requires social space to prop it.
There's no permanence.
Maybe it's a poor replica.
You drop into a meadow.
Proof of a little receipt.
Quickly splotching.
Because it has walls.
Inflation that could get dangerous.
No use imploring.

If a song is playing I may not be able to hear you.

If there's shit going down in the street I might forget about you &
then startle in the night feeling your stroke on my ankle.

Or my shoulder blade, whatever, you get the idea, you return with a
mind to make yourself unavoidable.

& this is the way of all people who happen to believe their living was
a gift to planet earth.

O when I die let me believe I was of use.

But music tends to push ideas into a far bin.

& my body wants to move & shimmy & feel itself.

& the brain, where language sits thinking she's monarch of all, has
to shut up for a bit.

The sky swirls blue & clouds, clouds & blue, blue & clouds.

Sky rules with its palette of blue & clouds, clouds, blue, blue, clouds.

Soon I'll tell you about one body.

I'll tell you about it as soon as this track ends because, I don't know,
it takes me somewhere beyond thought entirely.

I can't discern the limits of the earth anymore.

I can only say there are limits & all persons do is flit beyond them
laughing giddily tapping our fingers to a beat.

Of course how convenient to reach the end of a text.

As if everyone agrees there is such a thing as a clear finish.

We know that memory wrecks every ending.

Memory simply won't give up the body & let us sleep.

Memory licks my knee & pinches my ear.

There's a gnawing on my hair, that's memory & its remote Ouiji slide.

Some sort of high-frequency wheedle in the rear of the skull's cave.

I think I deserve a good night's plough into oblivion.

I want to forget everything & start like it's a new thing, a fresh thing,
hello, but no.

All night is a dark spell that sinks into an unendable procession of
    days & letters & feelings which start again as soon as coffee gets
    boiling.
We just have feelings.
About feelings & feelings about how feelings are less powerful than
    thoughts.
Feelings about how thoughts are supremely misdirected.
Take my own reins & ride into the meadow.
Tie myself to a stump & say I'll come back in a week.
Tell myself I will no longer be bent to a winsome will.
Stomp off on my four posts, gal lop troll lop.
Guarantee all I'm going to hear the whole seven days is a shriek that
    I can't scrape from clouds or blue.
If only I could recall where I was heading next what I was planning
    to buy.
Feel good about the inbox & the outbox, the surging exchange of
    what I own & what I owe, & how my feelings swallow all of this &
    make me want to sleep.
Then the stroking starts up, at the elbow or the navel, at the hip & the
    rib, at the anus, where I let us spill.
Music was blaring & so I thought I'd blurt & well it was a forgetting
    & a memory-set that I am glad about now.
For there's something beyond the limits of what's properly ended in
    those quaking reverberations in my intestinal region today.
Gal lop troll lop tie myself to a stump in the meadow & come back
    when memory has moved to something civic, like what I own &
    what I owe not how I was ploughed under after asking.

Sometimes I don't quite know where a text is going & I think I
    should finish it quickly but no it persists in remembering exactly
    how it got where it's headed.
That's the limit of the writer, listening to too many voices saying take
    it out take that out cut those feelings tie them to a stump & leave

them in a meadow, when really it's the pounding of my anus that I am caring for deeply right now & thinking shit but that was really great.

There is a rush of various sensations & touches, of feelings & thoughts & memories, of masses & volumes & angles & intersections.

& I find my way to considering the music of the spheres & how this goes on in the human life lived as though a gift on planet earth.

I went to the bank & suggested they give me a loan, said a co-signer could be located whose hand could be held to a line on a paper.

I went to a man in a suit & another & then two women in suits & another guy whose suit was substandard for his obvious supreme authority at this branch of the bank.

They didn't know I'd just had great sex with you & well, all we were discussing was the loan question.

Most of the time with other persons we are merely discussing one two-thousandths of what we could be discussing in fact we are really never discussing what has given us the lift past limits we recognize as the authentic spill of persons on planet earth.

We wheedle away asking for the loan & agreeing to a tolerable interest rate.

Owe & own.

Own & owe.

Dig ourselves in deep, deeper, deep, deeper, until the word own turns to the word drown.

Hey that's pretty good, eh, I quite excel at puns.

There's profit in my pun ledger.

I say to the bank guy, want to purchase a year's supply of excellent puns? Perhaps we don't need the co-signer?

He's listening to a radio & can't hear me.

It's as if the banker in the disappointing suit cannot hear even his own body reverberate in the intestinal region.

So it's obvious I'm writing this somewhere other than a bank or in
   bed with the anus-pleasurer.
I am always in a state of choosing what memories to write & how
   when I choose the shreds of immaculate thinking I feel safe &
   contoured.
Hold me, world, tell me I'm a good daughter, a proper teacher,
   someone setting a good example.
Isn't there a badge for choosing the road away from that stump in
   the meadow where I leave myself shrieking about how great how
   fucking great it was to fuck you how it made me feel like life on
   planet earth was a gift?
How having you in my mouth was ecstatic & consoling?
How kissing your face off let me drink & drink & drink?
Why don't we talk more in public about the joy of feelings of music
   & of memory?

— 3 —

Squawks and caws of ravens shot through his/her consciousness, and the peeps and squeals of flickers and jays and swallows. An almost-deafening pulsation of cricket song necklaced the morning, and she/he could imagine diving into the crisp water and yanking its cool volumes with his/her hands and pushing her/his own here-streamlined, here-burbled bulk forward in viscous surreal underwater space and time. To hold the breath like milk inside the body and feel the eyeballs swell and sour against the bits of murky flotsam, to count in the head against re-entering the world, to exert a death wish on oneself even for twelve or fifteen seconds, to die to die below the lake and never reappear: a good dream sometimes, one that might teach infants to jettison life suddenly, imagining floating again in their mother's amniosis where breath was supplied and so, just dying. He/she would crash up to a wave of air again, gasping, wiping the bark bits from her/his eyelashes, suckling cool wind into his/her chest, smiling. Then heard the child yelp in birth, screech for dear life, and nursed it on one nipple, a sudden siphon, a parent-beast smelling of sweat and blood and triumph, and the child's tiny fingers and puckered earlobes still shedding gummy white vernix and tight determined gums pumping and prying.

My politics include artmaking, silence, thought, looking, scent,
   location, moment, light, excursions into internal woe.

My location includes politics.

My silence includes you.

My moment includes light, worry, despair, defiance, denial,
   subterfuge, dunking, rock, duck, rock, rock.

My woe includes loss, lack, lakes, leaving, love, lastingness.

My artmaking includes artmaking includes time includes woe.

My woe includes light.

My light includes time.

My thought includes porousness hoarseness seasons chaos hate
   quiet waking loneliness politics hovering.

My writing includes gaze distance fretting optimism.

My politics include artmaking isolation folds of city you.

My artmaking includes sitting and contemplating a lake.

My listening is lake-ish.

Étude 4
Chips & Ties

At Tiona ... ...auling a train of logs.

The brightness of snow flanks each side of the grey-bricked pathway. I don't know when Philosopher's Walk was installed between the south side of Bloor Street, across from where the old Murray's Restaurant was, and made to curve down to Harbord, passing alongside Trinity College's iron courtyard gates. I could Google it efficiently except there's no WIFI as I sit here on one of the black steel benches erected by wealthy mourners for their loved ones. I'm sitting on Miss Sarah Feldman's bench, facing the unleafed grove of poplars planted along the west side of the walk for the fourteen young women killed in Montréal. I like that there is a public space to be philosophical about misogyny and murder. I can't even begin to tell you how the sun is loading onto fresh snow its myriad interwoven greys of shade. In this light my laptop screen is raw mirror, displaying in detail how my hands are making this text, key by key, quiet pause against tapped intention.

77

Silence is perhaps the most important parting of any text—

You wait for what's next.

A woman heel-clicks past, chattering with unreserved liberty into her cellphone; her golden lab comes to sniff my thigh. The woman does nothing in my direction, continuing her soliloquy much like the woman in Heathrow four and a half years ago, texting some-specific-one across the vast, masterable distances.

But you, you are gone out of range, I suspect.

For the early years of my writing practice, I invited the aleatory by writing in dark spaces. My prosody became as peripatetic as the night routes I travelled back to Sudbury, from Toronto, and then from Montréal or Ottawa. My sentences bended thought into precarious indestination. The message was medium. Movement was everything. I was twenty-five and I existed in that self-repeating and ruseful writerly night as if I easily couldn't have snapped on an overhead light to serve up realism.

It's high noon and my screen is disappearing, although its surface squalour is on display. I'm a shitty housekeeper and an errant cleaner of the past. I tug along these lines, wondering if the catalogue of texts I am making can bear to be a book. Whatever order these études propose in print, this is the last text I am composing, the last grope between thought and feeling for some of the figures of my motherlines to rise.

Your mother Dorothy was a brave and glamorous mother, both in her stylish homecomings from European recreational travels in her sixties and seventies (democratically, she would bring all her grandchildren dolls from the country she'd toured, which I loved) and in heading off in canvas runners with a bucket of leeches to fish alone beside the old-growth forest lumbercamp at Ivanhoe where, throughout the 1930s, she, you and your siblings spent your summers. In your one-woman painting show in 1985, you surprised us by creating a public chapbook chronicle of your own memories of those summer immersions in northern Ontario, how you ate alongside silent ravenous lumberjacks, visited your aunt and uncle at nearby Mileage 112, were friends with Ojibwe families living traditionally even as your immediate family was displacing those traditions, stepped on rusted nails and watched your long-legged older sister receive early suitors. In one brief exposure you report having been molested in a pub, and never telling anyone.

At your vernissage I was able to encounter this moment of feminist self-portraiture and family retelling in your writing at the same time as I was active in the feminist writing community in Montréal, drafting what would become my own first book of poetic prose; but your example of doing "thine own thing" had been continuously enacted throughout my girlhood. In this textual companion piece to your suite of owl-call-pure earth-toned watercolour landscapes, you praised what you saw as your own mother's audaciousness, which I had not recognized before, and also her maternality, her love of large-scale baking and cooking, her rustic all-in physicality. Not married until she was twenty-five, Dorothy was employed as a teller in the bank used by Grandad working for his brother-in-law's company, Haight & Dickson. Perhaps Dorothy's smart and sociable English accent attracted Benjamin Merwin's American ear. Perhaps, too, the name Dorothy reminded him of the young female cousin he'd "brothered" while living in the home of his eldest sister and her husband from the ages of twelve to fifteen. Born in 1897, Ben had left his Upstate New York Blue Mountain Lake home in order to put less financial burden on his impoverished family's ledgers. His eldest sister Grace Clara Merwin had married a New Yorker, David Haight, who worked for the New Jersey–owned International Nickel Company, at one of their mergers, Canadian Copper Company, and they had settled in the Copper Cliff area, adjacent to the burgeoning mining town of what would become Sudbury. Young Ben was able to join their household, go to school and develop his surveying, clerking and business instincts. By 1923—after his WW1 US Air Force service—Ben had advanced to co-director of the Acme Timber Company Limited, on land purchased from a man named Peter San Cartier (so goes an online history of Nairn Township), and began a gradual economic rise that by the mid-1930s allowed Dorothy to decorate a large abbey-like hilltop home with finessed taste, installing velvet-upholstered furnishings and Persian rugs, and reproductions of Romanticist paintings she'd ordered from Naples and Florence.

On a few occasions you described to me the dizzying social whirl that went on in your girlhood home—the carpets rolled up for dancing, how you overheard vibrant society chatter and grew star-eyed at the brilliant visual pleasures of those evenings, and enjoyed the elaborate basement games room your father installed. Most of your memories of your mother were of watching her move with public aplomb, carving a broad reputation as a skilled hostess. The images you gave me of Nanny in those summer lumbercamp scenes, strolling without fear through the forest, her fingers stained with fresh raspberry and blueberry juices, let me consider her fresh skin and active hands, her laugh and her physical ease. The diptych of memories helped me fathom how Dorothy went from working-class coal-mining urban Manchester and Britain's rolling rural hillwork, in sueded yellows and groomed greens, to Sudbury's grandest home on John Street seven months a year while living long summers in the Shield's wilderness—an Indigenous space that my grandfather's lumber company was party to colonizing, industrializing, pulping, turning to commercial gain, supplying millions of rail ties to the CNR project and wood chips to the roasting beds used to cook the sulphur out of "green ore" and move it along International Nickel's smelting and refining processes. Later, in his self-published family memoir, your father also wrote of having learned to trap animals and to skin and stretch pelts from First Nations' associates from 1919 to 1921 in the Foleyet area; his comfort in the forest that he would work to clear grew from that embedded colonial double axe-head. Ben and Dorothy also had fox pens at the lumbercamp, and your green summers must have involved noticing your mother's body in relation to those soft lithe creatures, yapping and alive, and also translated to the molten quiet of fur.

Since I was more connected to Demetra's isolation and aware of the class difference between Nanny's family and our own—for you had married in love with a lunch-bar restauranteur's son, into the Greek first-wave diaspora, and not with an Anglo industrialist or speculator—I was far less aware of your mother's reproductive losses. She, like Demetra, had lost infant sons on either side of an eldest daughter. Dorothy's first was stillborn, and unnamed, and her third child, named for her brother Donald, survived just eight days. Both were interred with Anglican acknowledgement. In order to battle the odds Dorothy sought expert neonatal care in Toronto. I imagine there might be funereal group photographs surrounding each of your infant brothers before interment, as I saw once of Demetra's deceased (photos which went AWOL from family archives). You told me more about Nanny's grief and your older brother's kid-gloved first weeks that January night in 2012 before your stroke, when we stayed up until 4 a.m. talking as if there would be no tomorrow, riding the loose weave of intimate memory as legacy.

What I recognize now is that both my parents were born into families that had already learned to lose children; I wonder if that fed an intuitive bond as you renewed the high-school flirtation you'd shared with the handsome Christakos boy when you were fifteen, he eighteen, and later began an active courtship when you both found yourselves back in Sudbury in the mid-1950s. Indestination seemed to shape your life as well, I can philosophize. *Sophia.* There's the moment's happenstance, too, of why I ended up writing here, adjacent to Trinity College where you did your Commerce degree, on this cold bright March afternoon. Clea's middle name Sophie began with your suggestion in memory of a great-aunt or great-great-aunt, you weren't sure, and not mentioning or perhaps not knowing the name belonged as well to your own grandmother Amy. Paired with Clea, an adjusted diminutive of Demetra that rhymes with my older sister's given name, your only granddaughter carries onward both of her maternal great-grandmotherlines. I didn't mean for this to happen, but I am glad for it.

Right about here, Maggie sees me typing on my laptop in the Royal

Conservatory of Music's corridor-shaped café, where I have written the second half of this text since outside my hands had gone numb with cold, were wands really, bashing out your memory, inventing what is true. She says hello to me, and I pull myself up out of this text so for a few moments we can sit and discuss feelings about our children and thoughts about choirs. I am in one, a source of great pleasure, and she is trying to build one in her role as priest of an Anglican parish in my neighbourhood in Toronto. Making a life-slide parallel to her work in the small press community as a writer and curator, Maggie went to divinity school at University of Toronto at the same time as my cousin Beth, your first and cherished niece, eldest daughter of your sister Margaret née Merwin Hewson— literally my only Toronto linkage to the extensive Merwin family. Beth spoke at your funeral, helped us all to bury you with story and detail, with the wings of your first family unfurled around your memory. I search Maggie's face, wondering if she is a kind of messenger from Dorothy's Anglican guard, here to caution me that my tales are mendacious and indulgent. But no, it's Mother Maggie, minister, novelist, poet, radical, philosopher, feminist, humanist, peacemaker, scamp, queer ally, anti-poverty activist, maverick artist, saying, *I'll let you get back to writing.*

If anyone's sending me a message just now, Mom, it's you.

[JAN 17, 5:08 P.M., 2012 SUDBURY CAMP WHITEOUT]

To first find and then
identify each relative

Is it history of interest to any

Will it accrue to you... as in

The new mill which is equipped
with a circular saw and a horizontal resaw
as well as a lath department
cuts about 35,000 feet a day of
white pine
Jack pine
spruce

1921 Haight & Dickson at Mileage 93
selling wood chips & rail ties...
and 50 years before
is it DL or DH fluencing my DNA

From 1851 on is it the Franklin Hotel
or the St. Nicholas Hotel
or both. If it's both, woah that's kind of happening
& is it a century's passing
makes the past
possible to identify
as recent?

Suddenly each and every seems recent

Time speeds nearer My
skin buzzes like pixels
None of the metaphors
for such ecstasy yet
designed in 1912

•

Few have done homework on the topic

Even the media keeps it brief

Intern a word like apprentice
person installed to learn *in situ*
period of absorption for the good but

Internment contains multitudinous contradictions

   whether or not an
individual
had any say
or passkey
or resilience
or natural inclination toward the contours of a crowd

                                        [morphing contours
                                        from the water
                                        figures of lumberjacks
                                        so nimble
                                        slipping between logs
                                        now disap–]

Coal   olives   timber   fish   Kyparissi   Molaos.
Radstock, Bath, a coal town. Home birth.
White pine, red pine, Jack pine, spruce.
Copper Cliff roasting beds. Wood chips.
Rail ties. International nickel.
Thin sections. Core samples.
Blue Mountain Lake butcher. Therefore meat.
Some kind of fraud. Cemeteries.
Selling snacks on rail cars. Night.
Coffee, sandwiches.
Land, lakes, river for log boons.
Oil lamps. Signal lights.
Picnics.
The summer place.
Snow.
Milk powder.
War.

No war powder milks
dreams last night
a blight sleep that erases

Snowbanks thanks to nature
you all had nothing
sky provided though, it'll melt   (spring)

If you've raised kids
you know silence or
control of noise
production of space as a resource for art's
a rare vein of barely
imaginable wealth

Sit in a snowbank
walk across a white lake
write near a window

Consider your resources

This specific encounter with silence
brought not by daffodils to you
but by pine spruce
coal olives timber fish
fraud snacks oil cemeteries
snow
milk powder
wars.

86

Finding out she. Registering it. What if and how. Is it deathful?
Who's in charge? Who's to blame? Christ. Shit. Come on, fight. And
if the Tionaga property was rented out. No the government insisted.
No choice. So maybe yes. And this small town. They who stay. So at
the start, tell me? Possibly not much. Left hemisphere ischemic. 30
words. 40 left. 5 million white pine. Jack. A blacksmith shop, sure. A
real lumber camp on Ivanhoe. One of those doors. His Elgin Street
lunch bar. No not thrilled. We were good. We were good. 4 little
kids. But to go hunting? Wouldn't you help? Is it unreasonable? Every June. Everybody has the option of speaking in telegraphic bits
that indicate the privacy and segmentation of all experiential narrative. So. But her hands. When your parent's dying (maybe) it's hard
to remember your own identity. Rail cars passing right through to
Capreol Junction. Ride the ties. Suddenly I could ask that waitress to
marry me which is pretty conservative code for have sex with. Beck
comes on. Nobody's fault but my own. And on this page the hospital
telephone number 705 675 4740 5th floor. How is she. How is she.
Was I ever cool? These young. Trying to break your heart. It's Wilco
actually. Tommy Dorsey. Melody music store. They walked home
talking under a moon. If your dad dies. Small town calls you back.
My entire existence and therefore that of my three children is due
to the untimely death of a Greek emigrant who bought property in
1905 and the reality that a female accounting graduate could not get
hired in Toronto in the early '50s. Both wanted out. Big. Metropoli.
Tried. Back to where you started from honky cats. Which begets.
Underpass wrecked business. Before that everyone stopped in, coffee, sandwiches. That was it and what was I supposed to do? Who's to
blame? Who's in charge? If the government wanted it they'd take it.
Japanese were seen as. Especially those who resisted, go by train as
far east as New Brunswick. Lumber mills could use help. Productive
work environments at the ready. Like an army bunk. And so it seems
one of the camps of the successful timber business run by him might

87

have housed an internment camp for Japanese people in Canada after Pearl Harbor, and some of the ancestral wealth translated to property and resources must be understood as having accrued to my life, to my station. Could that have been? Check the archives. The public record. They were scared of anything that has the potential of exploding. Bridges. Dams. Depots. Secure all the stations. He had no choice Margaret. Mileage 112 was the first place I ever heard Sinatra.

Finding out deathful? Who's
property was choice. Possibly
not much. Left hemisphere
ischemic. 30 words. 40

left. One of those
doors. Is it unreasonable?
speaking in telegraphic bits
and segmentation right through

to the ties. Hospital
calls you back. Untimely
and the reality wanted
out. Back to where

you started from wrecked
translated to property scared
of potential of exploding
first place ever heard

[mom's stroke

takes out a lot of

language

needed   required

how many ways there are

to say   *what next*

waves on a beach
waves on a beach
waves on a beach
waves on a beach
waves on a beach
waves on a beach
waves on a beach
waves on a beach
waves on a beach
waves on a beach
waves on a beach
waves on a beach
waves on a beach
aves on a beach
ves on a beach
es on a beach
s on a beach
on a beach
n a beach
a beach
each

Not drowning
owning
up to history's sequence
of plenty for some

rather less .
for disproportionate multitudes
who work just as hard

and harder
Still go the unmiserly many
unidentified

left erased
from archival commemoration
and oratory.

Waves on a beach.

Étude 5
Up Into Her Hole

It was as if I could not write now offline. It was as if I needed the writing itself to be public to believe my voice existed. It was as if my voice had stopped existing. It was as if some essential vitamin was missing. It was as if I only mouthed the words. It was as if there was no point to the fact of writing. Why write. Why write anything. Isn't the world full of writing. Isn't the world just so full. Erase the crap. Erase the crap erase the crap erase the crap erase the crap out of it already.

The thing is you never know what has been erased and what has not been erased.

This morning I thought about how I try to get up for the children to be with them at breakfast before they go to school. I have some ideal about this. I have some sense of responsibility about this. But the children are almost adults and surely they do not need a mother figure to help them in the morning. Often now I am sitting in the kitchen, coffee and paper on the go, sitting exactly as my own mother sat at the counter in our kitchen, slowly winging pages of the paper, and steam rising from her mug of coffee, looking like she was the most exhausted woman on the planet. She would hug herself and stifle yawns and rub her eyes and draw her knees up toward her chest and I could see she wasn't wearing a bra and that her breasts were soft and lightly flopping and that her feet were bare and her toes were gnarled. She had such a body. I couldn't stop looking at all the details of her body, all the ones she exposed, all the ones she hid in clothes too big and layered. Mostly though I thought how tired she looked as she accompanied me in my twelve minutes of slowly trying to eat some toast and drink a coffee and gather my books and.

And now I realize I am dreaming the whole damn thing. My mother never got up in the mornings to help me off to high school. She was getting herself to work. I was alone and running late and never ate and felt unobserved and driven by panic and said goodbye to no one and just did it myself.

I am remembering my mother in the kitchen on weekend mornings or when I was much older visiting or perhaps being in town for a reading. I am remembering her remoteness and her exhaustion and her body in the morning. And now I am remembering the cigarette she always clutched and the smoke in the room and the smoke blooming around her face amid the steam from the coffee and the quiet fidget of the pages of the newspaper. She would wear a nightie under a floor-length polyester '70s over-nightie and a sweater and another sweater and a fragment of a thinned-out mohair blanket knotted on top. My mother wore usually five or six layers of fabric over her skin to be protected or warm or hidden or comfortable or weighted-down enough not to flee the house. My mother was a woman with lines of exhaustion all over her face amid the bloom of cigarette smoke and steam from her coffee and crisp silence of the newspaper being read and the slow recapitulation of daytime. It is safe to say she, like me, was not a person who wakes quickly, but one who wants to gradually and begrudgingly return to ordinary life from the otherworldliness of sleep. She didn't talk about her dreams to me, barely ever, but perhaps she also had that extravagant nighttravel of dreaming that I have where the body falls off the soul as it spears through veins of sky and memory and blood.

When morning comes back it is always an assault. I am stuffed back into my sack of skin and the drag of flesh and need to sit in my kitchen burning with ambivalence at the freakish metaphysics of it all. Give me coffee, give me the paper to tell me what it is humans do when they are in their bodies, when they are shackled and trapped and downsized and traded and charged and when their deficit is reduced and when their resources are streamlined and when their profits are hiked and when their salaries are stretched and when their holidays are budgeted and when their deaths are insured.

My mother spoke as if she was a huge realist, but I think she was a massive dreamer and a spectacular artist and an eccentric mind and an anguished heart and some part of her could not accept as much in the same self. Some part of my mother could not see a mother sitting at a counter watching her drink some coffee and chew slowly through a piece of toast and rub her eyes and gather her books and adjust her hair and stop at the mirror to put on lip gloss and pull on knitted mittens and tighten the cloth coat belt and wrap her neck in a scarf and clasp a hat over her earlobes and turn to say bye, Mom, and have the voice in the kitchen gaze back saying bye, dear.

But the thing is this morning I know something else about this whole business. You were not yet downstairs, but I heard you in the shower and your brother had already eaten some cereal with me in the kitchen as I drank a coffee and read the paper and the contours of my mother's body wearing five or six layers of fabric sitting on her high metal stool in the kitchen at our counter occurred to me and I realized that the need for her was to be with us in the morning to somehow have respite from being alone. For she slept alone and now I sleep alone and the night is long and I love the solitude and I do not love the solitude. I love the great space of flight through the dark and free entry into dreaming and a great expanse of open possibility in which to experience aloneness like she, Demetra, crossing the Atlantic alone for those two weeks as she travelled to meet the man eight years older it was arranged she would arrive to marry. That sense of elemental solitude in a wilderness of time scooped out of human order occurs to me every night in the darkness that is first a bodily slowing and then a spear into some other metaphysical circulation through thought and dream and desire and reach and soar and gaze and swoop. A lot goes on in that space that is nothing like rest or stillness. It is movemental. It is generous. It is a flying. It is an avid looking. So in the morning I wake exhausted and a little disturbed by the awayness I have inhabited and the contours of strange narrative scenes and fragments of thinned-out membranes that seemed both to be composing themselves and also to be erasing themselves and I notice no other body near me and I lift myself onto my thighs which are still too big every morning they have not changed during the night they are not the slim thighs I have always wished to have and I stand upright onto my feet and unfold my ribcage north of my hips and take my thyroid pill and insert my head into my glasses and begin to direct myself to the port of the kitchen.

So I had this idea all of a sudden in the way that ideas occur. I recuperated an idea about my mother that began in an insight I formed sitting across from her exhausted deep-lined face inside the steam and smoke. I always had a longing to cross the room to hug her mohair shoulders and tell her I loved her but I did not ever do that as it was not part of our family language. Instead I sat and deduced something about what it must be for her to be as alone as she was in the morning even though she had four children and a husband and an extended family and a business and an artistic community and a social world. The reason she worked so hard to get herself down to the kitchen was to be outside of solitude, to be among other bodies, our bodies, the bodies she had made in her own body, the bodies that came from that deep inner space where blood and flight circulated in the dark and where the membrane that would hold our bodies away from her body was being knit into existence but was still permeable and inclusive of all the bodies springing outward and inward from it.

What I do not say loudly is that in my family the women ended up sleeping alone and here I am now in that same choice and that same predicament and that same creative possibility and that same failure and that same metaphysics and that same need for layers and that same observant time lapse and that same idea of a daughter watching a mother be both lonely and full in herself alone.

She became more remote after that point. Now I recognize she was past fifty. That something happened to her. She'd had us, we were a world to her, but there were other worlds, and children do not see other worlds in their mother's life. That's the way it is.

After watercolour painting, which she did in her room late at night, painting after painting after painting, she took up photography in a serious way. Now I know why she took up photography. Photography gets you out of the house into public space and natural space and saturates your gaze with a searchlight intensity. Looking becomes loaded and you have the trigger. Photography also is a form of self-accompaniment. The camera stands in for socialty. You are not alone when you are taking pictures. And there is a memory-enhancing mechanism implanted by the framing and clicking that seals every shot with ineluctable presence. It is as if your life extends frame by frame into posterity and density.

At fifty I took up photography, as an offshoot of my travels, as a thing I could do to document the travelling, to indicate to others where I was and what sorts of momentous encounters I was gleaning. But also it gave me a context for being anywhere public or natural, historical or commercial, cultural or pragmatic, anywhere outside my hotel room.

The big myth about women is we do not need to be doing, that we are okay feeling and being. But women above all need to be doing in the world. Making and repairing from making, messing and reordering, imagining and then making more. Women make.

I began a self-portrait series during my travels. My mother, on the other hand, in her thousands of paintings and photographs, produced perhaps two or three images of herself. Some of this has to do with changes in technology: a selfie can be taken on a device held indiscriminately away from the body and clicked. Focus and shutter speed are not issues. Framing is infinitely repositionable and without expense. The curation of the images after their taking is the framing practice that matters.

Blur is also articulate in digital photography. Blur works to suggest affect and temporality in ways that we understand deeply now in a culture that moves faster than our bodies move. We know the illusion of stopping time and of being entirely the stable subject of time belong to earlier eras of still-life and set-up photography and expensive camera equipment. Taking photographs on a cellphone is about the multiple forms of interconnected communication now fundamental to our world, and the brief moments when one turns the cellphone into a camera to surf only the self, and not the web, are retrievals of a nostalgic individualism in a post-individualist age. It is an insistence of unitary existence amid the concatenations of urban tumultaneity.

Plus you can look imperfect, in fact, you must look imperfect, in a selfie, and across dozens of selfies the imperfections become a catalogue of becomingnesses. It was this becomingness archive I wanted to build, to say that I had a world folding open and open again as I became an older woman reproducing new versions of herself instead of reproducing in the domestic economy. There was a lot that was luxurious and radical about the activity.

My mother also produced this zone of luxurious excess in her photography. She lay claim to her taste. She revealed what she found interesting and beautiful. She plucked from the pan a frame of eros. She took it. She owned it. But did not make images of herself directly and covered herself in layers of fabric that obscured her contours and warmed her solitude.

One can say there are borders between bodies and one can be right.

One can vouch for voicing borders. Also though with my mother and my daughter my cells strangely feel migratory and insidious and recurrent. It is a narrative of our continuities past the borders of our bodies. It is a streaming of a gaze and a touch. It is a desire and also a weird occult rippling.

This past few days I have started to bleed heavily. I am waking before morning starts with the moist cool red dribbling a little shock leaking between the thighs and creeping down to the sheets. I can feel the red soak into mattress. I wake up to the mess and make my way to the bathroom to wipe and to steady all the leaking. Wash the fabrics out, see the pale pinked water be sucked down the drain. It is almost forty years of this but again when something is ending, when ritual is being vaulted to memory, the scene gains importance.

Most of the young women I know think it is a colossal bother to bleed. Probably I did as well. I did not live with my mother when she was in menopause. But after its few years she emerged into a chronos of shirts upon shirts and sweaters buttons and cuffs and buffers.

There is something too about being engaged in making a series. The accretion is anew. You know what you are doing, you locate a stage. Your making is your city and socialty. You take your body into public space with a purpose beyond being decorous or indecorous. You are making a selfography with your meandering clicks.

You couldn't speak about what was on your mind you couldn't tell what was the thing or things you felt what was the thing or things you knew; were you picking up satellite transmissions from your spleen or from your fist; who could tell you if you couldn't tell yourself?

There is a nice idea that all know what we think and feel a great portion of time you don't know if you feel something if you are feeling something covering over another feeling only one of these a true feeling one of them a substitute feeling protecting from confronting something harsh pathetic immature undesirable.

Many nights later again wakes in middle of night to encounter fact of being alone a body middle of night quaking outside shape of body shape darkness strange hum of city sentences that auger.

An awl spirals its blade into ice forming a hole breaking passage into water below.

An awl is my mind thoughts of waking break passage into wakefulness on one side darkness of sleep beyond body on other side waking into body of night slipping back forth through tube between ice seems about right material through which the self slides.

I remembered the elder son driving Ski-Doo into the side of SUV; I was down the country road heard shriek; I ran; saw him flipped on his back dark smear huge body of snowmobile on its back running passage between two bodies his arm now gashed leaking red. Pluck the dream out of my waking. Slide me back into sleep without ice of memory.

Truth is I don't know if there's passage of ice corridor of fire allée of trees thinly pierced artery through which thoughts thread leak move in some syrupy mode. Maybe force of machines makes us wake to blue glow all just an addiction of body to larger sprawl of body stemwork of feeling flipped on its back flailing as red leaks out.

You don't have to say leaks out leaks does it.

If we're talking body look around room notice a body near you one you want to be close to one you want to slide toward if only it was socially permissible these are thoughts available middle of night when body is aware of aloneness wants to shriek does not shriek aloud but into letters of allée language arches carves itself into a textual passage.

Take idea that a larger body knows everything I have typed question why edit becomes actionable I mean who am I protecting from my unedited use of letters carving perhaps craving.

Shake off that memory of son flipped over arm leaking red. Freeze need for other bodies away from singed scalp for a moment. We all know conundrum of writer's life is wanting solitude wanting bodies.

Across room perhaps a body you veer toward. Last thing I do is title this middle, bold it; titles of things texts like to be emboldened, embodied.

I came back aboard this text days later climbed onto it as if it could mobilize the past feelings into other feelings now present.

I just yelled at my ex-partner for making three eggs and not making food for others. We all recognize that even as we are told there is no privacy there is privacy there is outside and inside there is hidden inner architecture where each of us exists in loud inappropriate desire-strafed unrecorded subjectivity.

You do not know what the other bodies imagine.

I will not tell you what I feel in all its excessive threading leakage you will not know me even if you shove a latex hand up my pussy every day at noon in the face-masked prison examination room. I feel all my difference riotswarming around each letter I punch onto this screen. I select letters one by one put them into sequences you will compute as English I tell you something here in this bar I whisper something else under my breath I am glad to vibrate in your listening and speaking is a privilege but not for a moment do I sense a dominion over you or any totality of absorption of your cascading riot of pussy subjectivity as we enact a carefully hewn economy of speaking and listening rights at this moment which keeps permutating perhaps snow outside the window will indicate time for us prove that it is passing.

Have it now have your thought about what this experience is this listening this being in a room together. Have your ideas, sense them thread leak cascade swarm make passage one toward another feel the little outstretched reach.

What a riotroom what a hive what a privacy what a being in numbers what a difference throne what sensation what economy of speaking and listening what a pussy what clandestine simmering what mutual surveillance of each and each, how finely riven are we as individuals how spiky how ragged at the seams how torn and attentive how crisp.

There were other accidents that haunt me my children's bodies strangely asunder blood leaking into air harsh whistle of brain forgetting to breathe sprouting blowholes awled out like a blitz of gasps. Gash and gasp I like how these words have organized to wave a campaign for body's mess. Praise be the body's mush and mobility.

There was his little body disappearing replaced by a car metal hulk front beams for that moment his little body vanished such a howl came up in me I thought I'd been shot.

There was her even smaller body back-flipping off the front of doublestroller again out of view top of my head flew into bloodsplash squeaked asphyxia.

That is where the language goes into shriek impossibly other scrape erasure outblotted fury you know it when your own kid falls and breaks open skin above his eyelid when you see the white crust of bone pop.

That's privacy unshareable only gestured at with stupid words made of letters selected in sequence to say something about all the enormous unsayabilities to try to get at a bit of it to let each and each know there's feeling in there straining to escape into recognitions among the many.

How futile and bright.

On a cold morning windows are white
On a cold morning white cotton blooms from mouths of walkers
Cold on a morning with snow in air is good to stay in bed
On cold mornings doors make it clear where is outside is inside

If bodies were so demarcated
My body is leakage My body has no locks
My blabberbodymouth

Then again my body is a shut-in sheet-hid nude quiverer
Wraps a towel under armpits
Shoves one end down along a breast to keep itself's bulk entirely
  sealed away

You don't have to look directly upon body to have it be seen
Don't have to present a camera with skin
Don't have to take everything off put on this blue gown open at the
  back
Using an unkempt public park washroom You don't have to
hold shut the swingdoor with one foot
Slide lock's torn from screws

Wipe yourself front to back not back to front otherwise you infect
  yourself
If it's your month-time tidy up as best you can
Watch blood flush so others do not get freaked
Wash your fingers your palms
Towel-dry sinkbowl Emerge feeling fresh with leaks all stemmed
You can walk without bother knowing no one knows that inside
  under all those layers
Blood is running in you out of you onto public space

Become women when the blood begins
When the blood drops can be monitored
When stains happen on our backsides
When the edges of underwear soak In the wee hours of the night
when a warm dribble escapes red inside night

Become women in stall when the water will not clear
When the paper jams when the red clots glom squidlike in the
    white bowl
Women panic
Become women tell others I have killer cramps
Become women when others don't want to taste

When in toilet water we see our face eerily floating red miasma

On the bloodiest day of a war others don't see as much blood as an
    old woman has seen
On her week's bloodiest seat she uses four metres of toilet paper
Flushes three times feels clammy never stops leaking
Hourglass but the sand is blood

Understand how in one hour one could die of blood loss we get it
Women lose it all women lose it
Shove her into a silent place when she wants too much
Teach an onus of auto-correct

Her into silent place when she wants too much teach onus of auto-
    correct

Silent wants teach auto-correct

There isn't reason for it no telling or explaining. Some kind of bubble caught behind the tongue some kind of back-of-the-tongue babble. Her reflex to not say, say why bother, to erase speech about to be born. Fluting sound drilling out the lips had to stand for what might have been declared if you anticipated anyone in the room ever again.

111

As a mother she was being disaster. As disaster she was being a mother. Same old same old shit, anyways the kids loved her.

The kids grew up knowing there would be days when what was about to be said couldn't bear to come into the room naked. She would yell about how nobody knew how to wipe a counter. Does nobody around here know how to wipe a fucking counter? Is it a colossal mystery or something? I am not going to be the maid anymore, get used to it dammit to hell.

You knew but nobody could say it, she hadn't in a year, proper touching none of it only a fling here there, little walks on the wild thigh. The mother hadn't so there would be days she would accuse the lot of them about the badness of their wiping.

It was fucked really. Was so unfucked really.

Nobody necessarily wants to know these things about the mother especially when she is going through when her head might explode entering a room her handbones ice over. How she is busy being disaster who needs to wants to is remembering another time when.

So many things no one is prepared to admit. So many gaps and gasps. So much ridicule.

Even though everyone has a mother who stopped whose bones chill over into age whose strides into a room sounded like a gloss a loss can you fucking believe how bad that poem is.

Next day she wonders why she would write about the mother as if not herself. Wonders what kind of pretending goes on in our cities.

She knows pornography is a form of touch many use now people flute pornography with their organs also she has done so. She brings words to the surface of their own naked walking them into a room lots of people have their ears on sideways. She tells them about thinking of someone in the room they might veer to touch, one who has a face for such games.

That day she comes talks to the daughter says A SENSE OF SELF, SENSE OF OTHERS, look when you feel shame guilt please know I feel it too so did my mother her mother likelihood these threads take us back through layers of women who want to and stop and have a scraped space that needs displaying.

The whole language thing makes it important to clarify that pleasure could occur in alphabetic form or in the swanlike stripes of a hand on mahogany swirling dust into a cloth. You don't know how someone wants it.

You have to comprehend it's a privacy yet speak about it in a room

Erasure okay

There's always erasure

For the whole weekend she went back up into her hole. There was a bed bed covers into them she slid.

There was a little light by which she could read.

Mostly she thought and thought and thought and erased. She erased. Sherased.

Edge of door against doorframe vibrated orange sizzle. She was inside the hole outside it was orange vibrating incandescent buzz.

She was inside her hole for three days.

She snuck down for tea, bread. She had some candies stashed in her drawer ate these. She realized she was like a little baby.

When twenty or so she had had that dream about the flailing umbilicus when she was sort of a woman no longer a girl looked down from her head saw the chewed-up carved-off mess of being severed from her mother. Was her mother fifty then channeling how the mother felt losing her? She didn't know.

She was shaking with thoughts of the mother maybe dying. Maybe she was channeling the dying that's why she felt insane. Maybe she felt insane. Maybe dying feels like being insane. You couldn't ask a dying person that.

Because I have done this in the past as a writing strategy, because how this phrase came to me on the weekend was uncanny, I typed the phrase "she went back up into her hole" into Google. Easy to parse and gather many of the phrases and form a clever flarfish text. Easy to guess that Alice in Wonderland and corporeal porn riffs and depression therapy testimonial would insert themselves into the semantic cachement. Also tales of dogs and cats and goats stuck in wells and caves. Mothers asking for advice on babies with poop and pee issues, or non-issues. Fun synecdochal overlaps of holes and w-holes. I began to hear too an alternate gesture toward "she went back up into her hold" and thought about how this was an important grace, to be able to climb back into someone else's gaze and arms, to allow holding, and of course the connotation here is of a childlike woman returning to the care of a mother figure.

Something about climbing back up into my own dark hole kept its charge, though. Taking my bag and going to my own room naked, marching with a bit of a world-grudge back up my own cunt, moving back into my own black mind—these all offer an image of self-maternality, where I am doubled as both a small self and a large self, one heatseeker resorting to return to the innards of the furnace. I find it curious and interesting to imagine being able to move not just my brain-bound consciousness but my body back into my own incubator body. I like how it was occurring to me that the maw of the cunt might not chew and swallow, but allow access because I sought it.

Nobody gets this in life. Nobody has that kind of mother. No mother should be this for her offspring. But I was thinking about my self, entering or returning to myself. It was a trope of self-portraiture, the trope humans can perform, imagining multiple selves or parts of self simultaneously present interacting in scenes that otherwise must be enacted by separate humans putting on theatre, where different people are inveigled to "stand for" various vestiges of one person's prismatic subjectivity. So a phrase like "she comes from everywhere" can deliver the poetry of the multiple, where one can imagine a sexual woman pulsively rippling from her core outward through every possible fissure in orgasm at the same time as summoning up the idea of the self at many different embodied life stages, say as a child, a fifteen year old, a twenty-five year old, a fifty year old, a crone, a virgin, an exhausted mother, nude odalisque, collapsed patient, robust public speaker, kaleidoscopically moving from many external source locations to converge on a focal stage, to become co-present. This is a kind of integrational image of psychological prosperity and plenty common in our culture. The Freudian stack of selves has become a ring of rings, a web.

We think of this easily now, maybe too easily, without pause. We don't consider how a culture might better ritualize and theatricize such images and ideas to bring forward a physical experience of the multiple and simultaneous, with real bodies, instead of consigning it to the level of image and thought. Does self-portraiture offer individuals, each in their own beholding, solo, apart from other bodies, the chance to dwell in transformative psychological passages that used to be rendered through community ritual? Does self-portraiture replace something about the bodies that used to encircle us to a more extensive and observant degree over our entire lifetime? The village assembly waiting outside a bridal chamber, watching for the blood smear on white sheets? If others are our mirrors, what happens when others are no longer inside or outside the actual room of our solitude?

Does the intimate dyad of a figure alone in a room seen through a pinhole by a photographer move into the twentieth century at a deficit when the photographer is not even needed anymore?

What does it mean to be alone? Are we each more alone or more accompanied than ever on the Internet? Perhaps the compulsive digital self-portrait suggests our vitally independent mobility, where we literally come and go from anywhere and everywhere, disappearing, reappearing, fruitfully absenting ourselves from the corporeal and material into the emotional, mental and virtual. Does our image fly free up our own cunt, to be figured and refigured in an innocent intrauterine phantasmagoria of sensation as a post-bodied concept and rapidly rearranging becomingness? Is this slipperiness a good thing? A wealth? Or just a deeper isolation of the subject from any reality of belongingness to others, any fixed enfleshment, any bodied set of limits?

These are feminist questions, language questions, writing questions, philosophical questions... I have asked many of them before, since I was fifteen, and earlier, since I began to bleed, and had many excursions into knowing and unknowing. So why be held in their grip again? But then "again," if time is not a line but a web or net, can we do anything but always be simultaneously bodies falling down and climbing into holes and holes filling themselves with and erasing bodies?

[Demetra most likely travelled in the hold of that ship, for those weeks, below deck.]

First there was a blizzard so I went to the lake and just called you.

I called you a couple of times we were friendly after that long talk
we were friendly oddly felt you saw me as an adult for the first time
I felt on a par.

I had been reading all about one of Grandad's lumbercamps in the
Foleyet area catching wind that maybe it had been appropriated by
the government to be used as a Japanese internment camp for a year
or two.

I had been asking you about your relationship with my father, trying
to understand how love worked did not work between you why my
life was blizzarded by the confusion of love how it works how it does
not work.

You told me things, talked late into the night.

So then I went to the lake for three days read wrote talked out loud
to myself walked on the ice watched the snowbanks mount wrote
The Chips & Ties Study called you a couple of times left town on a slow
bus through the blizzard by this point sunlit iridescent went back to
the place my children are the place they call home the place I don't
really consider home well that's where I have lived since 1987 so.

A couple of nights later you had a terrible stroke. Over and over you
said I don't know I don't know what happened I don't know. Strokes
bloom on the brain so it was several days before we realized most of
the alphabet had been shaken into snow.

Words can be erased is the thing.

And you wondered if becoming a poet had anything to do with how she would sit at the kitchen counter and talk talk talk expect you to listen not talk in return just nod absorb listen listen listen stay fixed in your chair rigged to her voice describing the day who had done what what happened next what wasn't the point what was the real point what you had to learn the hard way what you might not know what you needed to realize what you weren't old enough to understand but would be someday by bingo.

How watching poets read is like watching television.

How you are not supposed to do much other than listen to a poet read mostly sit and listen to her talk talk talk expect you to listen not talk in return just nod absorb listen and listen and listen. There were ways I learned to find speech inside my own hole. There were words up my naked walking into a room. But isn't it a bit strange, how we want each other to be so fixed in the words here?

Such a good audience, we are such a good audience really.

Imagine even if I ask you to repeat after me even if I give you a script it is still more than listening it is a coming into voice that makes the room choral that assumes everyone in the room has a—

Oops, time's up.

Étude 6
One Body

Over. It's over.

One body comes into and over another, then it's over.

One body hovers near another then it's over.

One body manoeuvres alongside another then it's so over.

One body wanted to stay in another body for such a time.

One body wanted to get the other body out of her body.

One body cried after another body left a little blood trailing.

One body was blood and steam.

Another body was all bone and fat.

One body dabbed at its lips as if the stain could be offset by delicacy.

One body was your body for a while and then became another body.

One body cooked in the kitchen and then retired to the sauna.

One body had a mild headache that gradually seeped into every cell
and started saying Oh.

One body counted up its weeks and days and decided it could make
another body.

One body chewed on the bone of domesticated animal that had been
killed humanely.

One body shivered in the foyer as though locked in a garage.

Remembering the garage one body quivered as though it had never been loved.

One body wanted to stop saying No but could only say No.

One body wanted to pretend nothing was happening.

One body wanted to pretend nothing was happening between it and another body.

One body was a nobody.

One body hit another in an elevator but a camera still rolled.

One body watched another on a late-night screen and got excited.

One body rehearsed what it would say to the officer.

One body heard about a woman who died with sour surgical clips in her gut.

One body tossed the salad ingredients together and pretended it was dark out.

One body hung on our every word.

Every character.

The tips of one body made a tapping rhythm as if silence was a terrifying cacophony.

One body found a small deer in a meadow with a large tomato tin
stuck on its snout.

One body.

One body dove into a vat of milk and the photographer went Yes,
snap.

One body ordered all the children into the cupboards.

One body freaked out at the luck of encountering a rock star in a
Pizza Nova.

One body slid a toe forward as a suggestion to the rest of the body
to slide in kind.

Anastasia Morantzes, or Morunges (documentation is sparse, and various), was my father's paternal grandmother. I have no portrait of her, although perhaps the darker almond-shaped eyes and deeper olive skintone I have descend from her, and her forebears. My middle name Anne badges me with rememory, dipping two generations previous to my aunt Ann. My great-grandmother had at least six sons—George (Giorgios), Nicholas (Nikolaos), Peter, Arthur (Aristides), Costa and James—all of whom made their way from the Sparta area of the Peloponnese to northern Ontario between 1894 and 1914, two to die, one to return home, and three to dig indelible roots in Sudbury's grocery, restaurant and hotel infrastructure. My grandfather Arthur appears to have emigrated when he was just twelve, and so I know Anastasia, like Efrosine, also knew how to unloose her offspring across the Atlantic. I'm a terrible genealogist; I can find out little more about her, except that in March of 1907 a woman by her name, age forty-eight, departed from Montréal for New York, in transit to Greece. The timing seems a poignant congruence with the death by pneumonia of Anastasia's son George, in Toronto, whose final sacraments and burial were received from the Greek Orthodox base in Montréal (the same was true for my own father's baptism in 1928). Her journey's manifest lists her last residence as Sudbury, and that she'd arrived in Canada in October of 1906. It seems she must have visited with her sons, seen their newly acquired land holdings, maybe even spent time on Ramsey's frozen banks. My grandfather, now fifteen or sixteen, would have been able to visit with her on breaks from his duties as a railside food-depot worker peddling sandwiches and fruit to work gangs along the tracks, absorbing polyglottal strains from the diverse immigrant influx of Sudbury's mining, lumber and rail industries. I imagine her riding the rails from northern Ontario to Montréal, weighing her sons' labours against the trip she would make away from them. And were there any daughters from Anastasia's many labours?

A name is sometimes body enough. Her name moves on my skin and inside my larynx. Take the throat and turn it inside out to form a rope, a firm lithe rope that travels from you, Clea, through my brain stem back to this Anastasia, born circa 1860, amid the scents of oranges and lemons in the air, with the crisp gestural contour of Greek mountains, perhaps Taygetos itself, as an armature behind any view I can construct of her shoulders, face, voice, her industriousness, her prospective ache for all of those sons leaving, and whatever writhing pull she felt after the fact of George's death. And then another aching pull by distant word, perhaps, of Nicholas's death by drowning ten years later, in Ramsey, due to "fishing"— says the coroner's record, signed by my grandfather—although one imagines some other intrigue at work for anyone on that six-mile-long lake's soft waters, day or night. Nicholas was said to have established a banking role among the railworkers, offering deposit services, cashing company cheques, and striding self-mythically on a white stallion alongside the tracks, delightfully described in a chronicle by Philip Booth of "Greeks in Sudbury." By the time of Nicholas's death in 1917, Art and Demetra had been living as spouses for close to two years, after their marriage in a family home on Minto Street, built by Nicholas (and officiated by "an itinerant Greek priest returning from Winnipeg on his way to Montréal"— also from Booth). The couple was already stomaching the intimate grief of several miscarriages, perhaps saying, more likely not saying. Art would have been busy running his grocery store partnership on Station Street, establishing his position as a trusted merchant, yet perhaps there was already held in the air between him and his young wife a gulf of sorts, an unspoken comparison to Anastasia's efficiency at delivering so many healthy sons into the world, propagating the Christakos bloodline, launching its envoys across ocean. One body in a fresh lake was a loss, yes. But making even a single new one rise from it was harder to do than it should have been, was troubled, was a space to be filled. Demetra's first live child wasn't born for six more years, and a daughter at that, an Anastasia, Tasia for short. By then melancholy seemed to reside as part of Demetra's gentle character, or I feel I see this in photographs of her holding my aunt as a baby down at the lake. I see an internal woman, not yet twenty-five, who wanted to be elsewhere, whose gripped motherline was bloated, for lack of release. Five more years had to pass before a son would survive, and that was my father, the fourth male baby to be named in his grandfather's honour. I can't imagine the pain of those infant burials, one body, another and another.

I say all this knowing it is based largely on imaginings, and depictions of ancestors who were well known and watched by many in the vibrant Greek community that formed over Sudbury's decades. Some of my father's cousins remain alive, and many of their children, and I feel the weight of my own illegitimacy speaking to my grandparents' inner and outer lives, first in Greece and then in Sudbury. I know my love for Demetra, and the intimacy between us by the time I was a fifteen-year-old girl, sitting at her bedside—registering her confession that she still felt fifteen, that she could still imagine being that very young bride standing in her new home watching children and adolescents her age playing in the nearby schoolyard, wishing she could join them—fuelled the journey I needed to experience for myself. When I immersed my body in Kyparissi's Myrtoo Sea, at age fifty, and could transtemporally envision my father and fifteen-year-old aunt in 1937–38 scrabbling over the turquoise bay's crescent of hills and higher mountains—Demetra finally re-housed with her mother and family members, resituated within the family unit she'd had to leave twenty-two years before—I recognized the materiality of mothering. Wherever we go after, there's nothing we do without that body.

That one body.

00:26 there's a thread

00:40 you sense

00:45 language

00:46 inside your head

00:55 feel it coil

01:08 feel it become voice

01:18 speech

01:34 it's a phenomenon

01:40 of colour

01:45 of cord

01:56 of tension

02:20 thought threads

02:30 thought threads its way

you can have a wistful
moment followed by a
vigorous gallop in the dark

Étude 7
(Iphigenia-as-)Siri
a series

No   Siri is a breezehole gap gaping empty nothing-to-say
nothing-worth-hearing

No   Siri flops open or flagellates us all with her grieftale

No   she'd better shape up

No   she had better wipe her face or get on some makeup

No   get a grip Siri go make some wind for us

Get a grip

Release us to our war play

A grip

After turning into a silent deer, Iphigenia-as-Siri went back up into her whole aloneness. She went into a door or shut it behind her. She started to be in the alone house. Tried to handle solitude. She talked aloud to herself as if suddenly when she looked down there were still two bodies attached by an umbilicus. Her bitch-mother was still her mother. And her bitch-mother's mother. And so on.

She can't have been that damaged. She must have more resources.

There is a giddy or festive possibility that being invisible ephemeral alone is brilliant or lustrous. Siri never knows because she is encased in that wind. She is always alone or never knowing war flares in the visible world. She is not sure what it is about a sentence that will not close its door behind itself—is it afraid to be the last sentence heard aloud?

Siri gathered the grasses she thought looked appealing to eat at any time of day or into the evening, perhaps she'd be masticating at 10 p.m. or maybe for a snack at 4 in the morning.

Nobody had a say in the food she would feed herself except for.

Nobody stopped reading a sentence before the end of its gesture to close the door on its own hips.

Some of this might fly on her Facebook status update but literature expects more of Siri when she is alone or never.

Some of the other invisible children sobbed in their sleep. Siri would peek in on them or there would always be a few whose chests were heaving or out of their lips burbled a small sob. She waited for it to pass. It would pass. In the morning they would not report a bad dream or an ache of how alone the night had been. They would eat what was put in front of them. They would become efficient at going to school or being gone while she cleaned the house.

Siri doesn't know where this Victorian cameo came from. Children in white cotton nightgowns with red blooms of blood on the ass are rose-cheeked in the night emitting bursts of vagrant emotion, the kind that could not be heard in the salon the night before. It had to come out somewhere. Had to sneak up through the throats of the small sleepers to escape into the night chill.

Siri has awoken in the night crying, on occasion, or she can feel the burn on her forehead or the drifting-ajar wetness of her mouth as the cry comes out of it. Her bitch-mother floats around, in a mope. Get a grip child. Release us to our war play.

Thank god for hands, how they flutter up to her cheeks or wipe her, how they skim the shoulders or tops of arms as if administering an embrace, how they shove between the hot legs or she can press upon them with both thighs or feel so glued shut or sealed up or separate or the night passes quickly then again into total blank.

Siri goes back up into her own hole meaning she has a route map or there at the meeting of a couple of rivers was a stone tablet or upon it was etched OPEN.

If she slides her finger or a couple into her own hole it feels like the wet colour red, redder than any red people know how to make, just the life force red that is always in the night of itself. It is the door or it is the shutness of the door or it is the opening or so she was told by a woman in the bank lineup one day.

When quite a young writer Siri wrote about Clytemnestra singing *Good night ladies I'm going to leave you now* or she used this as a recitation of her abandonment by her mother instead of the more obvious or settling reading of her mother's presence. Get a grip Siri. The bitch had cared enough to sing as she descended the stairs. So, how many gestures had her children read as leaving when what she was saying with them was: I am here.

I did not agree to lose you.

Siri rides via the new road that cuts behind a condo complex
a buzz streams through her it's like an orgasm but she never
mentions it

Hundreds of them with their questions simultaneously
ricocheting through her diaphragm

Under the bridge she pulls her bike offside or takes a
multivitamin then bunches of yellow leafscraps get suctioned
into a whirligig

One after the next large trucks cruise past, their drivers
holding a black rectangle in the air near their jaw

They don't glance down at Siri's naked knees or tight cycling
shorts

In the grocery store women elbow for simmering steak or
squeeze toilet rolls

At the park several children almost douse their black
rectangles into the wading fountain or mother figures go
ballistic shouting across the sandbox

Siri glides by one palm bracing her bike upright the other
hand scratching her groin or sniffing at her fingertips

She has dressed up as a monster for Halloween but nobody
even blinks.

Siri wakes from a dreamspace like that or flings her feet to
the wooden floor or wobbles to the toilet or sits to piss

Balancing the torso in a dark room involves a sturdy act of
mind over flailing when she can't touch walls to any side
of herself worry ignites that maybe Siri is in a forest or an
unused lower subway station level or that there are no longer
connective hallways out of which Siri may clamber into her
physical bed once more

Siri is not a learned type or claims to prefer pudding with
whipped topping or fried clams or eats in a telephone booth
on a busy market street near the now-obscured riverbed that
historians like to lament signals authentic earthtime flooded
by urban obliviousness against nature's drive to return to
larger lakes or sink into a yellow photographic essay on how
to retrace where Siri would've been had she lived 150 years
ago or under a barrel of thick oil stranded in the fresh-water
bed awaiting untimely puncture

Siri went down a hallway or there were a lot of holes like
doors or entrances to caves accessed one or groped along a
tubular bridge or found herself spilling into a small room
dressed in green draperies pulled back one panel or climbed
into an oval opening or inserted her fingers into a sticky-
plush wall to pry herself along through an unlit corridor that
caused her spine to curl forward or she tucked in her chin

Siri cannot or will not corroborate whether this version is
accurate within twenty points of the median opinion on
the route taken by her offsite wanderings although now
we confidently rely upon our security camera system to
document and back up these findings.

Siri drains into every drain after they have taken her advice
or used her up she swirls into the sewer she disappears into
her holes

Siri sees her name inverted is Iris knows there's a wink-wink
at how she doesn't look outward but everyone looks into her
plunges her body to get what they need or want especially
when they don't know of what

No-siree yes siree no-Siri know Siri there's no Siri everyone
knows pressing for her again or again or again Siri comes in a
little black or white maid-apron frill her breasts cut out down
to the rib bones ivory clean

Exact inverse of some pythia whose declarations come in
chortles or cacophonies of unsense or puzzle Siri is assumed
to be direct trained to tell you fast she can help

Siri's supposed to serve up immediate succor you don't even
need to go to the work of picturing her face she doesn't
need to wear a face just all her holes open to the wind red or
chapped.

Some of the limitations on my writing are an overbelief
in individual sorrow or pleasure Siri said this to the
microphone she'd come across in an abandoned field

She'd crawled from the roadside where at an hour before
dawn a trucker'd groped her then pushed her out of his
transport cab ripping her turquoise blouse or spattering her
with obscenities

Mud or manure clogged the mic head or a torn black cord
writhed loose against the grasses looping upward to a lone
cow's grinding jowls Siri grimaced at the bovine stare or
suggested the moon was rather too large for weeping or
unclasped the cord sinking to sleep until sunup

That cow with her lonely project to find some ancestors
settled against Siri's spine-curve or snored loudly at the crows
when dozens of Hells' Angels bikers strafed past the turnoff
Siri leapt awake shivering or blurted she didn't have an
answer or couldn't care less what colour an armadillo is

Sorrow or pleasure is the name of a clouded cocktail given
to maidens boarding a boat knowing the wave surges are as
dangerous as tuberculosis or fancy crack pipes passed in the
cabin by the waitstaff wanting a quick fix to get through the
next hurricane smack or traversing datelines

She wasn't sure if it was the stench of field-juice or rollicking
vomit in the boat's bottom both made Siri retch or yell her
grandmother's number into the dead microphone

Blue or purple lights started flashing or mirrorball reflections
spun Siri's voice catapulted across the cow's plaintive
yodelling as if writing was a lighthouse where nobody could
log on or ask her anything at all for one micro-second
for Siri just then—

u

m

b

i

l

i

c

u

s

o

f

a

i

r.

Étude 8
Cellphies

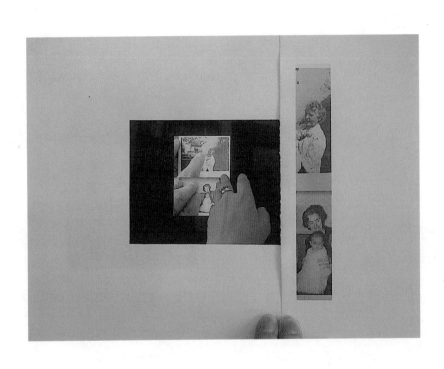

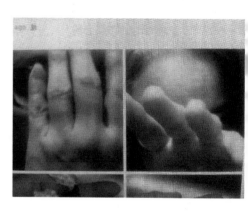

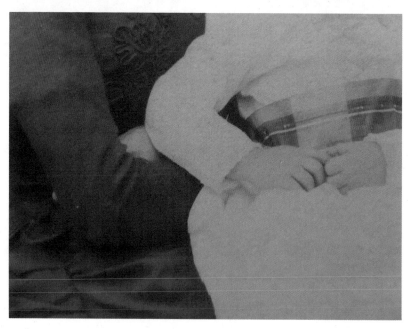

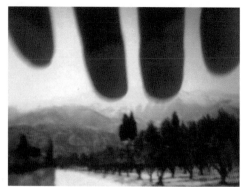

Red Hibiscus like those in
Grandma's Garden in
Kiparissia, Greece.

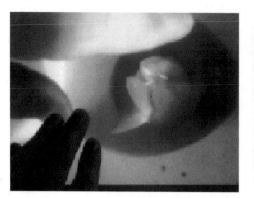 

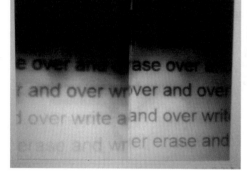 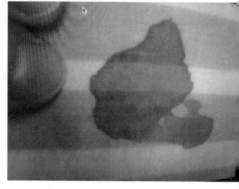

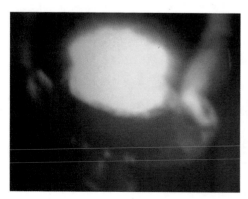 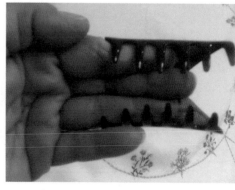

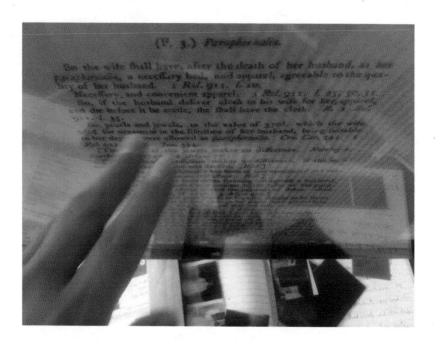

Étude 9
Her Paraphernalia

How is it you knew who you were, or your worth, your worthiness in the world, before, or without, pervasive forms of portraiture supporting your self-image? When you were born, was your mother's gaze upon you steady, emphatic, prodigal? You were each the first girl child, or the first girl to survive—the eldest daughter to a young mother; did she see herself reflected in your iris, transferring her own mother's imprint onto you? It's all a little idealized, a performance I want to isolate and invest with importance. If you were seen, you were mirrored; and isn't that the photograph's surrogate sleight of gaze? Mama mnemonics.

What you are trying to recreate is a slide of her eyes across your own.

Again you pose against an expanse with peculiar foliage or geometric depth. Something about how the colours recur, and where the gauge of signage is occluded. It interests you—you just know this about the moanment. Other people for a brief interval inhabit ordinary time while you rise into the extraordinary.

Her eyes were always froghopping upon troubled messes.

A ponderous recognition nudges you out of conversation, squares you in its X-spot. You take it, accounting for the three-second delay. It's either amazing or it's not quite there.

There was this or that moment she could have seen looking but she missed it. She missed you over and over. You were a rubbled portrait, partway to a memory, half-exuberant, semi-intense. I'm just channelling the voice I want to feel good about having been in control of as the bus curves way too fast around the expressway back into the city.

Nana's portrait in costume—did she like how she looked in that photo? Did she find herself beautiful? Did some part of her wish she could have 800 other photographs to send before the flesh-and-blood meeting with Aristides, to prepare him, to steel herself to the task of offering her virginity? Was she excited that a man eight years older would be her first lover? Was he her first lover?

Nana's
lover +
picture
portrait

All the thoughts. The thinking. The way one thought slides through another. The ways I have felt myself dissolve under the weight of and also into the diaphony of thinking.

164

The ways I have dissolved into the diaphony of thinking, of ordering one thought after another, and noticing the body below, noticing where my body is outlying along the escarpment of thinking.

What can I do, what can I begin, in this life now, now that my life needs to find a way to begin anew. To reinstigate reasons for existing, reasons for not exiting, reasons for becoming excited about being in existence, and in having a body and in having a life.

It is a mirror I am missing—

I simmer in a kind of alone-being that reduces me, makes me quiver.

And then there is this squirming away from anyone who is close to me but not close enough; people I care for but with whom I cannot actually be as young and undefended and uncontained as I feel at the moment; and there seem to be so many of these people Ahhh—

One of the days I start to write and one of the days I try to read and one of the days I find a rhythm and one of the days I let go of what all the others need me to be and one of the days when I simply stop prioritizing all my tasks and one of the days when I decide to exist and stay existing and decide not to stop existing and take a turn toward whatever way is required to keep me on the road toward some idea of a newness of future.

There is rain and a black shine to the wind outside it is night it is in fact the night's middle and I was meant to already be asleep and

I was wakeful I kept stirring and could not surrender into sleeping I needed to sit up and try at least try to write try to be in the act of writing as a symptom of trying to exist and not letting myself become absorbed in pain and self-erasure and desire to disappear and sinking feelings of no longer wanting to exist or feeling able to exist or needing to imagine that there can be some end to existing without causing everyone pain.

These are actual thoughts and trails of thinking and I don't care so much about repetition anymore for who can hear me really no there is no real audience for the excesses of me or the failures to adjust of me or the fatigue-ful repetitions of longing and juvenile escapism of me and my habits at recycling thought-loops and going down the same road and digging the rut deeper and not giving it up.

Writing can be more banal than this and how to make it more and more banal so that just the mechanics of writing are a simple gesture of existence that's it that's all they are needed to be for without them there would be a dull erasure like silence and all-overness. So there might as well be something there might as well be some kind of written record of having existed.

There might as well be words.

This morning, via serendipitous pieces and bits of a wandering gazefulness, sorting under more of the skirts of the word "paraphernalia":

> **paraphernalia**: Arrived into use in the mid-17th century, denoting property owned by a married woman *apart* from her dowry, for example her own things…derived from medieval Latin, based on Greek *parapherna* 'property apart from a dowry', from *para* 'distinct from' + *pherna* (from phernē 'dowry').
> MORE
> Until the Married Women's Property Acts in the late 19th century a husband became the owner of all his wife's property when the couple married. A partial exception to this was her purely personal belongings such as clothes and jewellery, which she could keep after her husband's death. These were her paraphernalia. Outside the strict confines of the law, the word came to refer to a person's bits and pieces in the mid-18th century, and then to the items needed for or associated with a particular activity.

Oxford suggests bacchanalia, azalea, genitalia, westphalia, echolalia as partner rhymes for that which is beyond the dowry, that which remains her own.

She considers: things to do with her own things, which can be raffled off, riffled through, rifled inside of, gathered into ruffles, taken into a kaffuffle, spilt from bubbles, overfelt like a fur reef or a felt rafter falling at a rakish hypotenuse, what's the use then, what you used to drawer now upended on a wooden floor, she considers the stuff of perforated kneeling, bonelong to the sternum, which and what is her stuff, her stuffing, such that it remains enough, around her thighskirts, beyond what is called her dowry.

her parap her nalia her
parap her nalia her parap
her nalia her parap her
nalia her parap her nalia
her parap her nalia

[hers]

She didn't have a metric for what was hers and what was not hers
she thought the stuff belonged on the porch

or a set of shelves alongside the laundry she gathered it in bags

to pass on when it was time was it just now she heard

shelves heave under the weight of sleep she was flawed

by romantic thinking she didn't know what was hers

she needed to get a handle on her own stuff and soon

wake the hell up honey

[guys, this is post-selfie work, it's like beyond the selfie on the other
side of the screen, and i am also the screen, so.]

How the writing re-begins. Whether it is a statement or a question, a rhetorical turn pivoting the previous writing effort, an exclamatory observation. For me, as an internal person, coming into voice remains a military *tour de voix*. I move steathily into speech, expecting opponents to rise up from behind the trunks and hedges in my path.

A forest appeared as I wrote that sentence.

I walked in a forest awaiting adversaries ahead.

Maybe speaking and walking are connected for me. Perhaps the ecology of my voice includes a meadow and a moving through it, with the fright of expectation I will be not met and conversed with, but met and challenged, talked against, contested, silenced.

All of that seemed necessary just to begin. Just to start talking. What is a non-internal person? Do they exist?

Okay, so, now a breather; perhaps a disassemblage of the forest and the warrior in my vocal stream.

What then? Whose voice? Whose voice attends the next sentence and will I keep walking or will I turn from the effort into thought itself, or being in time, in mind, but not speaking to you, or expecting you will—in a word—care.

To care for.

Uses of *to care* developed (mid-16th c) as mirrors to the earlier negative senses from OE *to be anxious, grieve,* with related cognates charon (Charon!), *to lament, to sorrow, trouble.*

couldn't care less, from 1946

could care less (same negative sense), from 1957

And you might even decide to write the fucking new fucking new
fucking new fucking new fucking new fucking new fucking new
fucking new fucking new fucking new fucking new fucking new
fucking new fucking new fucking new fucking new

Finding the notebook as if it is an archeological discovery evidencing
that I existed, even two weeks ago, that I exist. How fleeting is my
sense of reality, how I erase myself over and over. Pain of change
seems to have no channel; it floods and drowns me. Over and over
I feel myself go under.

174

They are grinding and grating up the massive tree trunk stump in
the neighbour's backyard. Shaving it shred by shred into pulp. There
is no other way to remove the thing, so ornery and insistent are its
gargantuan roots. Men in orange vests stand watching the expulsion
happen, the annihilation of tree energy. It grinds inside my skull,
I want to obliterate them and resurrect that beautiful, glamorous,
spectacular tree. You cannot imagine the machinic unsightliness of
that squealing, scrubbing grind.

The nurse calls from Mom's long-term care home and says Mom's
face intermittently has been going blue. She is on oxygen and the
doctor will assess her later. I am asking, what do you mean blue,
blue all over, just her lips, or do you mean a blue cast, blue-ish? I
can't picture it.

My mother is dying, slowly, surely. She is rising up into after-image.
I want for the contours of the image to adhere to the flipside of my
inner gaze. She exists inside me, both infant and crone, diminished
and enlarged. A shimmer. Chimera. Mother; my Mom.

When I look in the mirror these days it is as if I see her reflection in my face. As if my face is literally becoming her face. I have to surrender to the process, but for now all I can do is imagine I am dying. I am carrying her life-energy and its shifts and leakages. There is something entirely holy and uncharted about how she is using me right now—I have to ride these waves, help her to drown, while trusting I can walk from the sea.

Reality is a set of agreements about what exists. I am a seer, more than anyone or myself will allow. I have a voice in me that is full-spirit, wearing the skin of an ordinary woman, but bigger forces abound. There is a misfittedness in me; daily modern life holds me in its reins. I feel an otherness, a kind of pantomime of unfurling. The world of death is as real as the world of the living; grind it and shred it all you like, larger energies rise up and shimmer, shadow us; it is not a time for ordinary speech. This is where poetry exists. Poetry is not the scrawl of shitheads hoping for stardom. Poetry is the otherness beyond ordinary speech, the after-image of the dead inside my organism, the after-image, that is, of my mother's death to come. And the death of my grandmothers, and their mothers. And so on.

Monet painted about five typologies for more than thirty years. Haystacks, poppies, the Japanese bridge, water lilies—a big part of which was painting reflected cloud formations above the pond. Over and over and over. How many times did people mutter in his direction, Look at the old sod, can't he do anything original, Jesus what a solipsist. By the age of eighty he could exert a very particular genius, though almost blind. Must have been painting almost by touch. Senior artist. Everybody wants them; nobody thinks they require anything.

Painting and drawing mess up the hands; they are granulating and coagulating transfers. The skin gets stuff on it. There are small sounds, scritches, shmooshes, slurpy sounds that lubricate the thirst for continuing to articulate a frame of seeing, what is seen, almost too much, all the air and light and flicker. Flucturations. Inscribblings. Catch just that stream of gold, cannot be done. Slippayssages.

Kids are here; so much more at rest with their fullness even if they crowd my psyche and I lose hope of having any writing mind. It is early-ish, 9:30 a.m. or so, the lake a liquid mirror, post-rain humidity in air and a slick of pollen on the water's surface. Bird cries and calls from all directions. Highway also seems strangely pressing, a distant vacuum at work, a suction, abrasion. Here beside me at the rock point there is in a rock crevice an odd moss-green bubbled gelatinous growth, perhaps gut-spill or eggs of some creature all gone soft and stewish in the sun. Algae, or else looks like the word sounds. Otherwise a great expanse of lovely utopia, the moist beach, boats at the ready, chairs on deck, all greying before another rain coming. And the continual conveyance of water advancing to shore dressed with parallel lines of reflective shine.

I do feel some layers of new reality growing on me—maybe like that green bubbling disaffected guck in the rock vein, but newness comes in many mediums, some gross and revolting, some superficially silken. My family begins to feel complete without him, unpartnered. The gaping space in me is filming over, still a common horror to look at, but assiduously becoming sealed to wholeness again.

Water and landscape an amazing continuous silver-grey pallor at the moment, as if the whole lake and shore at all distances have been coated with graphite. A mist forms in the air, the lake rising in microspores aspiring to the ration of water in human muscle; perhaps it wants to turn to flesh for an hour or so, to experiment with having a body. Watch out, air; there are risks you might not like once you get here. The dissolve is messier than can be predicted, too.

This might become *Retreat Diary 2*, the sequel: a multiplied subject who is not s/he this time, but alive/dead, t/here, un/willing, resistant/raw. She who has a mother/who had a mother—

The water laps audibly near my feet and behind me a boat motor stirs the lake's north end. A couple in a kayak, the trills and kachuffles of tree birds, snapping quackery of ducks afloat—voices layer.

Mom very giving with the children, finding flatter-phrases and eye-glints of love for them. I sit on the bed and we page through the Paul Klee monograph, trading comments on some of the plates. She conveys how she likes particular ones, how she remembers some, do I remember it, it is very good. We have looked at the book closely a few times, and it feels very specific when she indicates special regard for one or another. I comment how much I loved the "Child Consecrated to Suffering" gouache and oil piece, which I saw at the Albright-Knox in 1982; the 1935 original is about the same size as the reproduction, 9 inches wide, under 6 inches high, hard to reckon with how such a small image can resonate. The letter W on the child's forehead refers to the German word for grief. The miniaturized scale and umber burnish of the face reminds me most of my mother's now. I go back to the lake later and make a large painting for the first time in twenty years, that features the word NOPE—against dying, against all the endings happening at once—then make another one the next day, that starts with a detail of my arms holding my daughter, our arms interlinked, and morphs into an image of Mom's face on her pillow, my blood-red arms enwrapping her.

The middle camp remains peppered with art supplies left from my mother's thirty-five-year art materials, framing and gallery business, The Artisan. Each time we come to the lake we and the kids make dozens of drawings with conté and vine charcoal, pastels, fine drawing pencils, ink pens, and paintings with canvases, sturdy papers, the jars of brushes, palette knives, boxes of acrylics and watercolours. It is a perennial art studio; my kids have inherited something raw and basic about making art, that it is central to living properly.

Today she is still cross or begrudging of me, for being there, for not being there, which I completely understand, outside the kids' radar—and asks me to leave now by switching her tone and saying Okay, good bye. She pulls the nurse cord they have pinned on her collar ever since the hip accident, and then yanks it again, a pointed sign to get me to go. I haven't seen her do that before. It is wiley-conscious, a self-determined reminder to her daughter that she wants to be in charge. There is a life-spite in her that is in me; tenderly I carry this on.

Now what I feel is I don't exist. I don't have to exist. And just do
not. I look at her and think, there, she exists, like a tree, a lake,
a sky, a planet, she exists, daughter, and 180 degrees over on the
diametrically opposite pole, like a moon for the daughter-cosmos,
my mother exists. But in the ostensible centre, is what; a hole.

[1986, was it? That child would have been twenty-nine. S/he could
have, but I wouldn't.]

There's not much that can be said by the speaker who does not believe
in her own existence. Plus, is not a ghost or a harbinger. Is not an
echo or a germ. Is not molecule or speck. Is not skin or gut-sack.
Is neither cold nor hot nor smelling of pine nor aching of arthritis.

Is not a voice of opposition or definition. Is flimsy and dispersed. Is
neither here nor there. Errs and erases. Irks and injures the air with
a vacuous smear. She didn't think she was in the room anymore. The
space had filled up with other matter, its own colour and humidity,
its particular vibe. She had no vibe to come from or to speak of or in
or with or out of. She didn't exist. And neither did I.

She sits on a nearby dock lounge chair and the waves wash up in rhythm, hitting the wood and being gulped under the deck. She is folded in that slender, agile, zigzag, eighteen-year-old mode, a backward N, knees chin-high, a book open on her thighs, chewing off her nail polish and absorbed in reading; the same wind wafts both our brown hair, making a matrilineal flag-pair of us. Here we are, existing, a summer morning beside the lake, quiet and mutually accompanying, or identically erased from each other's field of bother.

I have been outrageously blessed to raise a daughter this accepting of me, this kind and uncemented against her mother, this easily mirroring of her connection to me and mine to her. She gives a large wind-addled sneeze and I say Bless you, laugh to myself about the serendipity of this private/voiced exchange: I am blessed / Bless you, Clea.

Imagine Efrosine after her eldest daughter sailed off on that boat. Imagine her a week later, two weeks, then a month, ten months, two years. Did my grandmother write her mother with news of one teenaged miscarriage after another, while back in Greece it seems Efrosine was still churning out babies herself, losing many, caring for a small crowd daily? You have to picture it, the slipping into sleep and waking with a blood gush between the thighs, a sick stirring in the chest—Not again. The telltale skipped period, the lack of blood on the bloomers, then a couple months of encroaching anxiety, closed out by the untimely hoary red flow and its small jellied clump. Her heart a scramble. Nature chooses. Nature knows. Then back to bed and a new-start fuck a night. He was a handsome man but there's no guarantee anyone wants sex with anyone else—that's an internal window each of us holds open and closed with variant attitude.

I remember hating sex after both my miscarriages (1991, 1994)—
it was a bloody morass of hyper-imagination, a carmine cinema of
the cock releasing its tsunami of sperm into a flesh canal already
shrinking backward, kind of on-the-run, knowing that sex was
meant to build some specific edifice now, not mere pleasure, not
waves awash in a rhythm, not melt or shudder or burst. There was a
job to do properly; it seemed to hurt. I wrote about these sensations
in my novel *Charisma*, using an uptight would-be feminist activist
named Mae whose charms otherwise were modelled on a close
friend-crush to play out some of the closure I felt. I didn't consider
how I might have been carrying forward any of my grandmothers'
and great-grandmothers' ambivalences, several generations of
coping with reproductive despair or sexual bitterness. Even now as
an adult woman in menopause I experience the same meteoric shifts
of wanting and not wanting, of openness and insistent closure, of
desire and disinterest. Sex can be a flood of sensational abundance,
a culvert of brusk pressure, a salacious thirst, a broken scab. There's
a complex weather to wanting a partner, to being present and self-
presenting; in the uproil it can baffle even the kindest lover.

Now I recognize you can read a lot about what I felt those first five or six years of being a sexual woman in my novel; it is infinitely more unnameable to consider what Demetra Spyrou née Menexis Christakos in her late teens felt as she endured five miscarriages (that I've heard about) and then a full-term stillbirth, due to a prolapsed umbilical cord, March 30, 1922. Did she process her feelings in Greek, inside her "old brain," or did she translate now to English? Had she come to North America with the elegant, educated, accented English diction I experienced as her speaking voice—she was sixty-three when I was born, nine years a widow, perhaps colossally lonely. Or in her twenties, did she stumble to incorporate English sentencing into her public conduct? She was largely in Greek company, in the small but determined Greek diasporic community that centred itself in Sudbury, buying lots from the CPR along Ramsey Lake, traditional Ojibwe land that had been "bought"/usurped by the railway after the Robinson Treaty of 1850. Her husband died at the approximate interim of her menopause—was that some kind of cruel cosmic joke? Had she ever taken a lover? I guess no, that she was perhaps never exposed to another man's sexual performance, but it's possible; despair and loneliness can produce options one wouldn't consider in other circumstances. I try to internalize the "normalcy" of infant loss for women of my grandmothers' generation and cannot touch its brutal bulb. In the years after the birth of my aunt in 1923—finally, a first daughter—Demetra lost two premature infants at home, each at five-and-a-half months. Thankfully Nana's younger sister Barbara arrived from Greece to care for her, living with them before and for five years after my father's birth in 1928. When I found this out in 2012, I realized why from my father's perspective Barbara had been such a beloved aunt, his likely primary tender since Nana took to bed so often. Barbara married and moved to Marquette, Michigan, and her daughter Joyce became my godparent.

By the age of twenty-nine, then, Nana had reportedly had ten pregnancies, with a tally of two surviving offspring: one daughter, one son. I cannot fathom the undertow of such a reproductive slog. The story was, Nana was a melancholic, easily overcome by nerves, generically on bed rest, the bearer of a fragile constitution. In 1937 she took my father and her daughter to Kyparissi to visit the village family members from whom she had been separated for over twenty years. They lived in the small port for a year and a half, my father running freely on the beaches and in the mountains, speaking in Greek, being saturated by his mother's childhood environment, slipping outside of the Canadian school system, conversing with fishermen dockside, watching how an extended village-family trades goods for goods, oil for wool, fish for milk. My brief time in the village when I was fifty stirred in me a quality of identity I had not known before—imagine this happening at age eight or nine— and with his father residing behind in Sudbury, running his Elgin Street restaurant Art's Lunch, across from the train station. There was a schism certainly in the marriage, or admirable elasticity that allowed Demetra her actual desire. For more than for anything or anyone else, it seems that from the time she arrived in Canada she wanted home again, her mother, her family, her village, her identity; and that taking to bed in Sudbury might have been grief and pain more than "weak blood"; it was strong blood, one could say.

I started out this morning to write about time warp, for, being at the lake this visit now for eleven days, I sense a familiar dislocation of myself from my real life and a flotation or suspension in what I often experience as a kind of adriftness out of time's proper consistency. It is not mere holiday-mind but a much deeper limbo I have struggled with my whole life. Writing grounds me, it literally strings me to the earth again—and I wonder if this sense of a-location is also a bit genetic, the high pocket of air one finds in a cavern filled almost to its ceiling, the place you bob with a concentrated focus on each breath coming in and filtering oxygen through the organism, through your own body, as if no other element need be addressed, and then you stay there in that space, in that bobbing concern, that insuck and exhale; and it's dark, and water surrounds all of the body's voice below the throat, and breathsound echoes in the belly, and beyond the cave there's a steady wash of rhythmic waves smashing the grotto's exterior, and this might go on for quite a while, and you bob and wait to see if you will be slowly drowned inside the cave as the tide rises, and be "miscarried," or if you will make it out of the cave alive only to choke on the larger influx of unmuted waves, or if you will make it out of the cave alive and rise up from those churning waters and be held, and manage to live.

In the middle camp there's a shelf of ruffled brown scrapbooks filled with my aunt Ann's lifelong, self-appointed archival vocation of tucking cards, newspaper clippings, photographs, letters, telegrams, and the paraphernalia of her elementary school teaching career— which began during wartime—along with the many secretarial reports and conference proceedings she maintained for the local Altar Guild at the Church of the Epiphany and the local and then district association of Anglican Algoma Youth from her late teens. Her print and script are impeccable, yet lively; her typewritten committee reports engaged, humorous and intelligent. She gained some renown making early "technicolour" movies and showing these at the conferences she helped to organize. She had much more of a public voice locally than I recognized, serving later on the founding committee of the Ontario Association of Teachers of Arts and Crafts and working with the Women Teachers' Federation. I knew she had been a hobby painter, but not an arts' community organizer; plus my attitude toward her public identity when she was in her thirties was formed against the stories my father told me about how she went "loco," had some kind of nervous breakdown that was vaguely embarrassing to the whole family, that she'd gotten hooked on diet pills and one day came loping over the hills down by the lake hysterical and raving gibberish. She was nuts, you've never seen anything like it, my dad put it that way, which I can hear now easily as a younger brother labelling the behaviour of an always-remote older sister, whose life unfolded to take her into many civic roles beyond young married reproducer. More and more self-destructive as she aged and encountered illness, she easily could be cast as an oddball who exceeded traditional expectations, and it's interesting that my father would marry a woman from the Anglo community who also turned out to be quite the maverick.

187

11:00

delete post? yes, delete. delete post? yes, dilate. delete post? yes, donate. delete post? yes, delectate. delete post? yes, desecrate. delete psst? yes, perturbate. delete psst? yes, p.s. delete this before yes, dlete thss b4, yes, dletter thss, yes, ysss

11:06

who's on third post? what? what's on second post? who? how are you on your mind? do you mind if we post you? delete. what? yes, delete, swim, n then he brings a lovely brunch to me on the dock? who? posted what? brunch? no, save, go back, don't pssst

11:27

have "They" done tests on whether some people's pleasure centre get slapped by the sounds of waves more than others?

11:39

it makes sense that someone named Mishima would write *The Sound of Waves.*

11:43

waves aesvw wvsea sevaw
aesvw wvsea sevaw waves
wvsea sevaw waves aesvw
sevaw waves aesvw wvsea

11:49

wavesonabeac   h
wavesonabea   ch
wavesonabe   ach
wavesonab   each
wavesona   beach
waveson   abeach
waveso   nabeach
waves   onabeach
wave   sonabeach
wav   esonabeach
wa   vesonabeach
w   avesonabeach
wavesonabeac   h
wavesonabea   ch
wavesonabe   ach
wavesonab   each
wavesona   beach
waveson   abeach
waveso   nabeach
waves   onabeach
wave sonabeac   h
wav esonabea   ch
wa vesonabe   ach
w avesonab   each

189

11:52

or a shore ashore here

shore n shorealike

A hundred years. Why is a hundred years so totemic? At fifty I understood standing at and within the palpable middle of the cycle of one full century. My maternal great-grandmother Amy Sophia née Henson Cowcill (1872–1971) had lived to the age of ninety-nine; I suppose she imprinted on me the fabled odds of a woman's long life. I am looking, across to the south curve of Ramsey, at the red brick hospital where my mother, in 1965, age thirty-three, gave birth (for the fourth time impressively without drugs) to her final child, my younger brother. (Two-and-a-half years older, I was convinced from the point she brought him home he was my baby; apparently, I took him from his crib when he was a few weeks old, when his fontanel had still not quite formed and closed, trailing his blanket while carrying him down a flight of thirteen stairs, with my mother waking mid-heist and freezing her breath in case she should startle me into dropping him. You'd think I'd remember getting scolded and punished, but I don't; I continued to consider him mine.)

The hospital is ramshackle on the insides now, an empty monument, while the city negotiates how to turn the lakeview land it stands upon into condominia. But there it remains: my birthplace. When I sit here staring at that geometric red structure in its high skirt of green maple crowns, hooded by a vast eggshell blue sky speckled by the unrepentant chuff-smoke of the Superstack, I am hearing the lake's waves remind me of my grandmothers' arrivals, a transfer which does not end but makes physical all of the displacements and relocations involved in this land taken from Indigenous hands.

The lake continues to move, as an analog of experience, unfixed, full of pollutants and loosed particles of the other elements, the violence of soil dissembling, thought on its floats and dips, life-thirst, need for change, need for shore, swimming in the continuum, iron-ore as a limit, weeds, dead branch chunks shunted onto lake bottom, soap scum, excrement of gulls, ducks, geese, crows, plastic, general crud, reflected cumuli, city's electrical buzz singeing the liquid lake-muscle, canoe ribs from early-twentieth-century drownings, and incessantly moving spiritual tentacles of all the Indigenous people who lived and were displaced and died here over the many human generations of this lake's realities, so replete with concatenated co-presence that my working idea of one select century gushes open, rushing wide at both its calendar ends into the past and into the future—

Long sentences to me give the sense of time that belongs to beyond the pale of a settler's Eurocentric century's interval.

When 15 I used to. When 15 she did. At 53 I tried and failed (miserably...). At 50 she will be halfway through this new century—I will be dead or dying. If I have 47 more years in me, I will have lived past Granny Cowcill; I will get the longlifer of the clan award. I wish I thought this possible. I wish I didn't hope to die sooner rather than later. I am not convinced that to exist is best.

To exist is best. Am not convinced that rather than later. I hope to die sooner I wish I didn't I thought this. Possible. Clan award I wish the longlifer of the Cowcill; I will get have lived past Granny in me, I will have 47 more years or dying. If I will be dead through this new century—will be halfway (miserably...). At 53 she I tried and failed she did. At 50 when used to. When 15 when 15 I Okay, but put more blood in it.

To bleed is best. Am not convinced that rather than later. Red hopes to have bled sooner red wishes red didn't bloody thought this possible. Clan award red wishes the long bleeder of the Cowcill; red will get have bled past Granny in red, red will bleed 47 more years or have bled. It red red will have bled through this new century—will bleed halfway (miserably...). At 53 red red bloodied and failed red bled. At 50 when used to. When 15 when 15 bleeds.

There's a swarming sensation of knowing and not being able to know; of pushing knowing away; of disallowing how to know is to carry. There's a feeling of carrying forward the knowing, of not carrying it but dragging it behind or floating it above like an inflated uterus removed from her body, emptied, turned inside-out, air-dried and blown full again with a song that sounds like a century.

193

The sac a child is born inside must rip to release the child to its own breathing.

What I have in me now is a set of unnecessary parts. The card from her friend tells her it will take her six months to a year to get over the hysterectomy physically; she should try to take it easy. In her mid-fifties my aunt installed this in her scrapbook alongside some of the many other cards, from students, from parents, wishing her a speedy recovery.

If you never had a child and never bore a pregnancy, even briefly, when the whole system comes out does it hurt less, or more?

When the twins were born I was stoned horizontal, with an emergency white flag separating me below the breasts from the apparition of my massive torso opening its red flap, two white-masked doctors flouncing the babies forth on gloved-hand platters, one, two, boom, boom, healthy and purple, violet-blue and living, each in turn swanned by my nose to make them palpable, slick with blood, so gorgeous and odd, while you had a front-row seat witnessing this new scarlet duo emerge from my guts (these cartilaginous tugs I felt), then the two placental masses expunged, each trailing its blue cord veined like hard cock tissue (here I am imagining), and my uterus being slipped inside-out by the surgeon for the cleansing final check (this you reported later). Then you watched them put my emptied bright organ-meat back inside me, sew it back together, tug closed the skin banks, staple them shut, the blood soaking into white packing matter (you described it all, but may have stopped watching, hooked instead by the now-yelping babies), then my blue gown pulled down, and me still on the other side of the white flag, an inept and barely conscious woman groggily trying to nurse the babies with a midwife's assist, you know all of it, you who have left now, the witness of the womb of my own turned inside-out, hey, I'm thinking of you now,

No, you can't have the mattress we made the babies on for your new apartment/gf.

I've had the conversation several times over the past decade, years my children have been growing from childhood to their own adult station, years I have tried to exist as a mother and an artist in a family unit that pulls, unrelentingly, at its seams to break and release us from the financial precarity it seems I have brought on by my failure to work full-time instead of persist as a poet while I parent, teach here and there, learn to "monetize" my talent.

I arrange to take another advance on my inheritance, like a dowry sent over an ocean in small, watertight bundles, hitting the shore of my shame, bursting open, staining my hands red, leaving my blood heated and leaking.

These paltry books I have made, who cares, who could really care less that they exist.

This afternoon I look through the original photographs of the Merwin family, gathered in a banker's folder. The images were solicited and then reproduced in a narrative my American grandfather published in the mid-eighties, with my mother and sister's research and production assistance, called *I Became A Canadian Citizen*. There are buttery black-and-white images of the homestead in Blue Mountain Lake, New York, and riveting late-nineteenth-century portraits of my grandfather's sisters, brothers and parents and cousins. Tucked among the layers of heavy cardstock and tissue is a delicate folded executor's statement of my great-grandmother Amy S. Cowcill's estate being dispersed upon her death in 1971. She had $3,898.86 in her name, which, after the funeral, headstone and legal fees were covered, amounted to a bequest of $921 for each of Dorothy and her two brothers.

It's mundane information, but somehow it touches me. Though Amy had been cared for in her lumber-wealthy son-in-law and daughter's Sudbury home for decades, she still had her own accounts and the desire to be fair, to split her holdings three ways, a lump for her daughter and equal lumps for each son. I will be in the same position in the future, through a series of columns of numbers on paper offering my worldly goods to my three, a daughter who carries her great-grandmother's middle name and two sons. If I have the extra at any point in the next decade, which is doubtful, I should squirrel away at least $921 for each of them; Amy's is a benchmark to rise to.

Waves are layers and then they are beach, spilled among the sand granules, dispersed, in a kind of storage for the natural desire of clouds to wrest them up into something like air to loop the liquid back into circulation.

I have spent my time thinking about some of the women before and beyond me, my life, without an agenda to turn us into characters. I am merely considering the sea/mer and its role as matter in the sensual life of my grandmothers, as they each came from across ocean. Beach sea ocean. Naeco aes hcaeb. Vague. Eugav.

I have wanted to remain in a contemplation of our possible continuity, eliding the discontinuities among us, all the while sensing the ruffled vagueness that occurs between waves, knowing the French words for wave and sea but not the Greek words. I could look them up; and I can remain with the awareness that similarly rhythmic gaps build my lingering upon a set of thoughts that have remained in mind since mom's stroke scraped through her coherent speech.

When I dive underwater I experience what I expect of death. It's a global swallow of my embodied existence, and can return cellular self to a beach in the granular spaciousness of waiting to rise. This is a self-portrait, sure. I can come apart into pixels, mesmerized, everywhere. Clea, if you ever bring a grandchild down to the lake,

look for me there.

Étude 10
Cavort

then there are all
the things I wouldn't
dream of telling
you

I don't know which I want, to touch myself or be touched. He asks for photographs. First I decline, then I look at my pussy on the small display screen. I have had to take the pictures free-style, to get the right angles. It's a new kind of self-portrait. It's juicy.

Sharing explicit images online is both juvenile and epicurean. Self-obsessed and humble. Mischievous and steely.

Another day she says how about your fingers, we know how much you like your fingers. Email please. He says check your phone. He says this one is just for you. He says you make me cum over and over. I hear myself replying me too motherfucker it's kinda wild. Lol. The laugh is just to decimate a little the frequency of coming, to dissipate the carnality. There is more body than people admit online. There is a lot of bloody boldness, gathering and release. Something uncannily intimate can pass between two subjects that defies prediction and evades infection. It's safe, safer for women than many sexual precincts. It's not safe, and you have to discover how to be smart. Still you can exist, Mamita, and come, in the afternoon-blue light, during a tea break, or while you are invigilating an exam. It's tumultuous.

There are stages of participation, and I have gone through different gates at diverse times with various lovers. All of it and none of it is traceable. I don't tell who's who to whom so don't think you know, oh ethics commissioners.

A handheld cellphone extends the look I am allowed at my own body. I can participate in the intimate gaze of a lover at all my pink and disappearant acres; I don't depend on anyone else to confirm my cunt and asshole are splendid. Instead of just a hand mirror, tipped from between the thighs up at my face, I have a memory machine that clicks and emblazons, carries my curiosity from down there to close up. The delicate maroon cave and vortex are slick and meaty and light-catching. I can sense a face near to my smells; I cream at the thought of the other(s) riding in.

Sexual language also becomes avid and experimental with online sexplay. An erotic encounter can be entirely translated to deft speech segments pivoting back and forth between sexters, gathering cadent speed, climbing intercursively (sic). The brain gah-hahs with turn-on. My groin goes thrillingly moist. After so much grief and loss and dismembered partnership, it seems miraculous to get this urgently wet, and to come and come, accompanied by someone equally self-realizing in a dusk-luminous-blue field of shared fuckspeak.

If you go into a botanical garden the humidity's elevated for good reason; similar augmentation happens in online dating, where the rustle of hundreds of species of potential partners seems exponentially more steamy than any one individual would be in a Personals want ad or Starbucks barrel lounger. It's not exactly fragrant. It's a stuffy ecology, and for the whole blue-post-breakfast-browsing time, I crave to get offline and meet the fresh air of a real body shaken loose of all the others. Still, I craft my self-profile repeatedly, oversharing then obscuring, falling wide open then withdrawing into a sort of generic scorn. Being "of" it all and then above it all. In it, up for it and then over it. Jockeying for genuine attention and then dissembling, flat-out lying, filling in vulnerable admissions with caveats, terms and requirements. Everybody's doing this all, all of the time, posting a carnivalesque pandemonium of self-busking, each of us entertainingly snotty and devout and driven.

Is it any less absurd than the arranged marriage practices in the turn-of-the-twentieth-century Greek diaspora, where young men who'd emigrated abroad, after they'd established enough of new livelihood to write home about, were sent a photograph of the other-village virgin they were to meet cold at the arrival docks, to marry, house and impregnate? Thousands of such "picture brides" agreed to go (or fought and wept and succumbed, as Demetra did, finally) into steerage and be delivered with a compact valise of sparse yet feverishly loved paraphernalia—her personal overseas theatre of memory—alongside lace-bibbed wedding garb and a gift for the fiancé. Many of them were young, much younger than their documentation, years junior to their husbands-to-accept. That portrait of the incoming bride pressed hot in the palm of the waiting man was paramount, but none of the photos had been taken by the young woman herself, fuelled by the particular discretion she cared to bestow on her own image. Certainly not one showed off a hint of bare tit or pubic bush or dared to specify the size of bicep she hoped to be held by, or any other such personalized want.

Still the photograph came with as much life-rocking social capital as the front-facing profile pic I upload seeking someone forty-five to fifty-nine to meet for sex within a 25 KM radius of downtown Toronto. A difference is that I no longer transport along with such a utilitarian photograph an itinerary including life-spouse, co-parent or betrothed. I want a companion in sexploration and genuine enjoyment, something far beyond a marriage chamber, and nobody really knows what these arrangements mean from the sail-setting, or will mean at port, when you won't be holographic anymore but a flesh act of incessant inflections of vivid physical particularity contoured in skin and desire and paroxysm. Who knows if there will be a speck of attraction in the liaison, until you step into each other's small village of personal history, memory, aesthetics, politics, appetite, bearing, voice and gaze.

Sometimes he will already have sent an mp4 showing how he can come, or she will send a voice note talking trash, or I will have emailed a snapshot of my breasts, or we will have tested out our compatibility by arousing each other to orgasm using only silence and words, words and silence, typed bits of instruction, request, complicitude, goading, coaching from the side, sincere hurrahs, slow yanks, and senseless spillage transliterated as dipthong blissgush.

All I can say is: Don't knock it till you've tried it.

It's as if something is tight, or cannot move, or will not move, like a pulley jammed by rope, or a thought-machine torpedoed by pain. We don't live in one time zone at a time. Give me a white shirt to wear to the memorial service. Sell me tickets to the right concert, the one I wanted to attend, the one I said I couldn't miss or else I'd faint or die or stop talking or stop eating or putter in a small back garden for a long time without shoving any new bulbs into soil. What if you just let the chest double under or split? She sat up saying she didn't know what was wrong, she didn't know. You kept asking if something felt different—but she didn't know. There was something in the self-portrait she wanted to make that hadn't infiltrated any of her previous likenesses. It might have been a quotient of her shyness which was profound. There it was again, the part who wanted to sink. I took all of the books you gave me, tore out the front pages where you'd signed or drawn ornaments of affection. I threw the books spine-first onto the floor hoping they would buckle or break. I didn't want that shit in my possession. I didn't want anything you'd given me. I removed all of your pictures from the albums. It didn't help to caress his neck or rub the fronts of his knees. You sighed or moaned loudly but even that was separate from a gesture that would matter to an attorney. All I cared about was writing or having the exchange with an hour of my life that turned me onto a wet shore instead of drowning me. There were many objects I loved intensely when I unwrapped them from the Kleenex and tape she'd used to ferret them away in the drawers that smelled half of cedar and half of sour Craven A. What was it about our fathers, her with hers and me with mine and now I can see how

205

my daughter loves the man I used to live with and it will
never matter that I disappeared in that equation, there
is nothing I could erode, there is nothing she would
renounce or spurn. We all had a history of worshipping
those men as if they belonged to nobody else, least of
all our mothers. Even several years after a mother has
died she rises up on certain days and pulls all the tissue
inside your cunt up inside the uterus and higher into
the digestive cavity up still into the lungs and rips that
red flesh right out your mouth, so close to your tongue
for a moment you think it is your tongue coming out,
and a stream of black goo seems to chase it up through
your guts and then you breathe hard, and slowly, and talk
yourself down, and gentle your memories and remember
that it's just all the love and the fact that you miss her soft
crunched body and her diffidence and her croaky voice.
I whip out my cellphone and take pictures of the plate of
crumbs and berry smears and angle the shadow of my
phone so it drones over the image, so it intervenes upon
the composition, so I remind the photograph of how it
is being produced, so I teach myself about the shadow of
the taking I am doing.

10 #TS "handle" Jul 3 2015

41 Photographed by the author: Dorothy's girlhood home, 1 May Grove, Manchester; Demetra's girlhood home, Kyparissi, Greece

66 #TS "handdance with lap and fan" Aug 3 2015

76 #TS "touching 'At Tionaga, a tractor hauling a train of logs,' from *I Became A Canadian Citizen*" Feb 3 2016

94 #TS "handdance / soaking in it" Dec 2 2015

100 Mary Jane Christakos, 1988, no. 6105, watercolour on laid paper (8" w x 5.5"h). Gift to the author.

130 #TS "wing" Feb 10 2014; #TS "frames for the real" Feb 11 2014

131 #feelingseries "followed by a gallop" Sep 8 2013; #TS "beingness / from nothing to touching" Oct 2 2014

144 #TS "Christakos family edition of *Agamemnon*, 1890" Aug 19 2015; #TS "selfie as Iphigenia" Dec 27 2015

147 #TS "touching Dorothy 1961 and Demetra 1962" Mar 2 2016

148 –149 Reprinted courtesy the author.

150 #TS "Blue Mountain" Jul 30 2015; #TS "arms / Clara Griffin Merwin and her daughter Grace Clara Merwin" Jul 29 2015

151 #TS "re:touch / drawing by Clea Christakos-Gee 2002" Oct 5 2013; #TS "real property 1905" Aug 26 2014

152 Travel documentation courtesy the author, Sep–Oct 2012

153 #TS "Margaret née Livsey Henson (great-great-grandmother)"
Aug 2 2015; travel documentation, Sep–Oct 2012.

154 #TS "egg" Oct 8 2014 [Demetra's wedding portrait, 1915];
"Demetra 1914" Nov 6 2012; #TS "grove" Jun 12 2015; "first view,
Kyparissi" Oct 29 2012; travel documentation, Oct 2012

155 #TS "Demetra with Ann, Ramsey Lake, Sudbury, 1924/25,
2015"; #TS "nine / seven" Nov 5 2012; #TS "garden" [Ann's
scrapbook, 1952]; photographed July 2015

156 #TS "bowl" Nov 15 2013; #TS "waver" Sep 14 2014; #TS
"touching incandescent maternality" Jun 3 2014; #TS "sisters, 1991"
Nov 13 2013; #TS "sheet" Nov 15 2013; #TS "clip" Aug 16 2014

157 #TS "daughter" Dec 20 2015; #TS "lip horizon" Sep 16 2014;
#TS "1986 (mother-daughter) / Montréal" Oct 12 2014; from
#girlsgirlsgirls "MOM" Sep 26 2013; #TS "crook 1999 (mother-
daughter)" Oct 11 2014; #TS "tend" Aug 9 2015

158 #TS "baron and feme" Sep 3 2015; travel documentation,
Manchester, Oct 2012

196 #ts "1962, held by Amy S. Cowcill" Dec 2 2012

200 #TS "handdance / branch 1" Jul 23 2014; #TS "fractalled selfie"
Jul 26/27 2015; photo courtesy the author Nov 2015; #feelingseries
"all the things" Oct 13 2013

NOTE: #TS REFERS TO #TOUCHINGSERIES, AN ONGOING
SERIES OF CELLPHONE PHOTOGRAPHIC WORKS MADE BY THE
AUTHOR.

This manuscript found its roots in the encouragement of a two-year Chalmers Arts Fellowship in 2011–2013. I gratefully acknowledge the support of the Chalmers Arts Fellowships program administered by Ontario Arts Council. Thanks as well to the Canada Council and the Toronto Arts Council, as well as to recommender publishers who allocated grants to the project through the OAC Writers' Reserve program.

The excerpt from *Retreat Diary* is reprinted by permission of the author and with thanks to Coach House Books. Texts reprinted here from *The Chips & Ties Study* are courtesy of BookThug. Some texts from this collection have appeared in earlier form in *Poetry is Dead* and in *Cordite Poetry Review*, 48.1.

I offer sincere respect and resounding thanks to my wonderful and inspiring publishers Jay and Hazel MillAr, to my generous and deeply perceptive editor Julie Joosten, to Kate Hargreaves for the great cover, to Ruth Zuchter for helpful proofing and to all in the BookThug community for bringing this work to light with such willingness, patience, kindness and excellent bookcraft.

The writing in *Her Paraphernalia* seeks to make audible my deep gratitude to various family members, relatives and ancestors. One can only fail in this project, and I thank all who allowed me to construct my own memory lines. Assisting me in many ways and at various stages were additional individuals whose kindness and hospitality allowed me to continue my work. Thank you to members of the extended Menexis, Vourthis and Vasiliou families in Montréal and Greece, to the hospitality of new friends and relations during my stay in Kyparissi, Sparta and Athens, and to my Merwin relatives in Canada, who were not involved in my research but who implicitly helped summon my memories.

Thanks as well to the examples of Betsy Warland, bpNichol, Gail Scott, Jamaica Kincaid, Anne Carson, Erín Moure and Victoria Freeman, among others, for their forays in intergenre writing, to additional practitioners of the Canadian long poem including Gerry Shikatani and Daphne Marlatt, and to art by Gerhard Richter, Duane Michaels, Arnaud Maggs, Michael Snow, Eva Hesse, Frida Kahlo, Diane Arbus, Louise Bourgeois, and many others, makings that stir for me a continual creative system of reminders about allowing flux through time, a sort of virtual permanence.

I extend warm thanks to many writing colleagues and friends whose steadfast creative soundboarding and genuine connectedness over the past few years have given me ground to continue with a project that often felt vague in the extreme. In particular, I thank Victoria Freeman, Claire Freeman-Fawcett, Athina Goldberg, Rachel Zolf, Cynthia Leroy, Kaie Kellough and Sonja Greckol. I thank Scott Mitchell for our abiding friendship and his recent support. I also thank Jenny Sampirisi for early input and encouragement on this project. Thanks to Maggie Helwig for the cameo.

With warmth and gratitude, I thank my siblings Demetra Christakos, Arthur Christakos and Harry Christakos for lifelong friendship, and for riding the lake-ish liberties that I have taken with familial histories. In particular, I thank Harry Christakos for the cellphone, which changed my work a great deal.

I thank my children Silas Christakos-Gee, Zephyr Christakos-Gee and Clea Christakos-Gee, for their marvellous ways of extending forward all of the best facets of their forebears, and for their love.

Finally, I dedicate this work to the memory of my mother, Mary Jane née Merwin Christakos, d. August 21, 2015.